Self-Discipline for Tedious, Boring, and Difficult Things

By Peter Hollins,

Author and Researcher at
peterhollins.com

Table of Contents

INTRODUCTION — 5

CHAPTER 1: TAKE CONTROL OF YOUR TIME — 11

THE 52:17 METHOD — 12
THE FOUR QUARTERS METHOD — 22
THE TWELVE-WEEK YEAR PLAN — 30
THE PICKLE JAR THEORY — 40

CHAPTER 2: TAKE CONTROL OF YOUR PRIORITIES/FOCUS — 47

ANTI-OVERCOMMITMENT FORMULA — 48
BUILD A PARKING LOT — 56
DAY THEMING — 64
HOW TO BUBBLE SORT — 71

CHAPTER 3: TAKE CONTROL OF YOUR OUTPUT — 80

70:20:10 TECHNIQUE — 82
MANAGE YOUR ENERGY — 92
UNDERSTANDING THE DRY PRINCIPLE — 100

CHAPTER 4: TAKE CONTROL OF YOUR ENVIRONMENT — 107

COMBAT UNCERTAINTY WITH CLARITY — 109
WRITE A TO-DON'T LIST — 117
BUILD A "GOOD HABIT MACHINE" — 125

CHAPTER 5: TAKE CONTROL OF YOUR EMOTIONS AND MINDSET — 137

RAPID PLANNING METHOD — 138
HYPERFOCUS AND SCATTERFOCUS — 147
FIND YOUR CREATIVE RHYTHM — 154
THE DAILY HIGHLIGHT — 160

CONCLUSION — 171

SUMMARY GUIDE — 175

Introduction

Why did you pick up this book?

If you're like most human beings, chances are there are two powerful forces working in you at all times: The first is the sincere desire to be better, to do more, to get organized, and to build a rock-solid life you can consistently stay in charge of . . . and the second part is the lazy slacker who would rather not bother.

We all want the laser-like focus, the discipline, and the sustained, focused effort that really makes a difference in building the kind of lives we want for ourselves. And yet, there's that lazy slacker in the background, working against all these high-minded ambitions. Isn't there some way to just ditch that guy once and for all? Isn't there a way to live an ultra-productive, successful life *without* having to spend so much effort?

In this book, I'm going to be really honest with you: Wanting success without effort is precisely the kind of slacker ideology that we are going to leave behind. The objective here is not to find a way for you to magically find hard work less hard, or to trick yourself into believing that the more disciplined path is the easier, more comfortable path. I'm not going to tell you that, for one simple reason: It's just not true.

Now that we've got that out of the way, here's the good news: Although learning to be more disciplined takes effort, it definitely isn't impossible. It's something anyone can learn to do, no matter how lazy and unmotivated you feel right now.

In the chapters that follow, I'm going to try to convince you that laziness and a lack of discipline productivity is not really even a result of too little effort—rather, it's a result of unfocused, inelegant, poorly organized effort. Namely, the problem is not that you don't have enough energy or willpower, but rather that you are spending it on all the wrong things.

Throughout this book we'll take as a given the following principle:

Being successful, accomplishing your goals, and being disciplined and focused means applying your efforts to the things that are genuinely under your control.

Being uninspired, unfocused, and lacking purpose and motivation means applying your efforts to things that are not under your control and never will be.

Let's take a closer look. Things that are (usually) not under your control:

- Other people's actions and choices
- Random external events
- The laws of physics
- The finiteness of time
- Natural biological limits
- And, for most people, the fact of needing to work, earn money, pay bills, maintain basic health hygiene, and feed yourself

Let's take a closer look at things that **are** under your control:

- When and for long you do things
- Which things you do first
- Your attitude to doing things
- How much you do
- How much you allow your environment to influence you

So, while none of us can control the fact that there are always twenty-four hours in a day, we can control *how* we use those hours.

None of us can control the fact that there are some annoying tasks and obligations we're required to do in life, but we can control *how* we do those things and the way we think about them.

None of us can control the fact that the world is distracting, chaotic, and demanding, but we can control what we pay attention to, what we say no to, and how we manage our path through those distractions.

Being disciplined is not about having an easy life or finding some kind of lifestyle cheat code that gets you all the reward with none of the effort. Instead, it's about the conscious, mature use of the effort you do have, and the **skillful use of your innate freedom to choose**.

No book on this planet can grant you a successful and accomplished life with no effort. But this book perhaps offers something a little better: proven strategies for making sure that the effort you *do* spend is done so in as smart, strategic, and efficient a way as possible.

If you're ready to start taking control where it matters, read on. All that's required is the willingness to take ownership of your experience, to push a little past your comfort zone, and to try something new.

Chapter 1: Take Control of Your Time

> *"Time is the coin of your life. It is the only coin you have, and only you can determine how it will be spent. Be careful lest you let other people spend it for you." —Carl Sandburg*

Can you control how much time you have in a day? Nope. But you can control how you organize and arrange that time, what you do with the time you have, and the order of your activities. In a way, being able to control these things **is** being able to control how much time you have.

First things first, good time management is not about juggling, working faster, or taking clever shortcuts. Instead, it's about the intelligent use of time. When you use time intelligently, there is always enough of it.

The 52:17 Method

Julia Gifford had always been fascinated by questions of productivity. She wanted to test out which approaches to time management produced genuine results and led to more productivity over time. She conducted a research study on employee workflow using the DeskTime app and discovered that the most productive employees tended to work with intense purpose for fifty-two minutes and then take a seventeen-minute break, fully disengaging from the task to prepare for the next work sprint.

Those numbers seem pretty specific, right? What's interesting about Gifford's investigations is how well it aligns with the Pomodoro Technique, which is a simple time management method that involves twenty-five-minute focused work intervals (pomodoros) followed by five-minute breaks, with a longer break after four cycles. Gifford found evidence that people tended to manage roughly ten-minute-long work sessions (two pomodoros) with a break between that was neither too long nor too short.

Depending on your current work habits, these numbers may seem surprising, either because the work interval seems too long or short, or the break interval does. Our expectations and perceptions of what counts as hard work can be extremely distorted.

Consider these two examples:

There is a task to accomplish.

Person A starts at 10 a.m. and plods on for three hours straight, no breaks. At the end of those three hours (i.e., 1 p.m.), the task is complete, and they're exhausted.

Person B starts the task at the same time but does it in "sprints." They first do forty-five minutes, then take a fifteen-minute break, and repeat that pattern twice more. They finish the job at roughly 1 p.m. as well, not exhausted at all.

Who is the most "productive"? Both took three hours to do the task, and both finished at the same time. But there is a big difference: Person A is exhausted, and Person B isn't. That's because Person B had forty-five minutes of rest that Person B didn't. In fact, let's continue our example:

Person A is exhausted by 1 p.m. and slacks off for the rest of the afternoon as a reward for working so hard. They've got a headache.

Person B feels fine and even manages to squeeze in one more forty-five-minute session later that afternoon.

Over the course of a week, Person A, who actually works "harder" and for longer hours, actually ends up doing almost four hours less than the person who is taking more breaks than they are. Let's continue our example even further:

Person A habitually finds their work draining and unpleasant—it literally gives them a headache. They're still logging the hours, but their heart isn't in it, and the quality of their work slips while careless mistakes become more and more common.

Person B manages their work comfortably because they have ample time to rest and recharge. Their work actually improves over time, and they get quicker and more accurate, producing higher quality work.

Yes, this is a pretty simplistic example, but the point is clear: **When you plan your time properly, less work can actually mean more work.**

This isn't cheating or magic, but efficiency—when you acknowledge that the human body is naturally inclined to function in sprints rather than prolonged slog sessions, you boost not only your output, but your health and well-being.

There's no point in "working hard"—that's for pack mules and slaves. By the time you can feel yourself forcing through tiredness, boredom, and lack of concentration, you are already losing quality. It's like squeezing a grape that has no juice left in it—you have to squeeze twice as hard to get half as much out. It makes far more sense to rest when you're tired, refresh yourself, and return to the task.

Being overworked also has negative psychological repercussions, some of which won't be evident for a while. You may start to resent your tasks and doubt your motivation to do them. It's a vicious cycle—the more tired you are and the less enjoyable the process, the slower you go and the more mistakes you make. You make the task harder for yourself. The next time you approach the task, you've already taught yourself that it's hard and unenjoyable and that you're going to be slow and make mistakes. So, what do you do? Push yourself to be "disciplined" and slog even more.

Go a little further down this path and eventually you end up burned out.

Instead, start to think of breaks as an intrinsic and equally valuable part of the productivity puzzle. Drop any programming that tells you that you need to push through fatigue, force yourself, or strain. There really is no moral element to it; it just doesn't work. Remind yourself that breaks are not rewards, they are not failures or concessions ("Fine, I guess I'll stop since I can't think straight anymore."), and they are not working in opposition to your goal.

You may be wondering why I'm emphasizing the value of breaks when most people feel like they don't work *enough*. Here's the secret: The two mindsets are one and the same. Being a procrastinator and resenting your work comes from the same psychological root as believing there's value in doing prolonged marathon sessions. Kind of like how starving and bingeing are not really opposites, but both different expressions of a bigger problem of disordered eating.

If you want to be efficient, be moderate:

Step 1: Work intensely for approximately fifty-two minutes

Decide on the task you're doing, set your timer for roughly fifty minutes, then go. Work with focused and uninterrupted concentration, avoiding distractions. One thing may surprise you: That fifty-minute mark rolls around a lot sooner than you think it will. In fact, the more immersed you are and the fewer distractions you indulge in, the quicker the work goes and the less tired you feel.

Step 2: Take a break for approximately fifteen minutes

Once the timer rings, stop completely and step away from your work (literally and mentally) to have a break. Use this time to relax and recharge. You can do things like stretching, walking, or deep breathing, but let's be honest—there will be times when this just feels like its own kind of work. You may find more relief and refreshment by simply switching tasks and going for a walk or jog outside, chatting with a friend, having a snack, or doing something you enjoy.

Step 3: Repeat

After the break, return to work and start another fifty-minute-ish focused work session. Depending on the task at hand and your overall schedule, you can comfortably fit quite a few cycles into one day. You might like to have a longer break somewhere in the middle, though, as you will gradually notice your energy levels waning with each successive cycle. This is normal.

A few words on this overall approach, however. You may be surprised to discover that you are so engrossed when that alarm eventually rings that you don't *want* to stop working. Being engaged in deep work can feel great—and procrastinators are sometimes surprised by just how much they can do once they've gotten started. But resist the temptation to do just five more minutes, even if you're feeling really engaged. From that point on, chances are you are only getting diminishing returns. Instead, pause on a high note.

If you're in the middle of something that is going well, leave it open for yourself so that you have something fun and interesting to dive back into once your break is over. When you come back, not only will you feel more refreshed, but you'll have saved a little momentum for yourself in the form of that easy task that is already halfway complete. This is far preferable to pushing on until you're at a roadblock or stumped by a problem. You'll be starting your break with all those negative feelings, and the first thing you'll return to after your break is a knotty problem.

Productivity expert and author Joan Bolker coined the term "parking on the downhill slope" to explain this technique. If you parked on a downhill slope, when you return to your car, the first task lined up for you is the easiest one—just roll out of parking and let the momentum get you started on your journey. The exact place you choose to stop and have a break can help you park on the mental "downhills" in the same way.

Bolker, who focused on students writing their PhD theses, explains in her book *Writing Your Dissertation in Fifteen Minutes a Day*,

> "You'll come to a point at which you start to tire and feel like there's not much left in your writing reservoir for the day. This is the time to begin to summarize for yourself where you've been, to write down your puzzlements or unanswered questions, to do what Kennet Skier, who taught writing at M.I.T. many years ago, calls "parking on the downhill slope":

sketching out in writing what your next step is likely to be, what ideas you want to develop, or follow, or explore when you pick up the writing again the next day. This step will help you get started more easily each day, and it will save you an enormous amount of energy and angst."

Here are a few more tips for incorporating the principles of the "park downhill" approach:

Do small tasks first: Start your workday with an immediate feeling of productivity and momentum by quickly checking off a task from the to-do list. The "low-hanging fruit" can give you a psychological boost. You may find that if you can just get yourself to do five minutes on a task, it's easier to carry on. It makes sense, then, to choose an easy, small task to do in that first five minutes as a kind of warmup.

Create "pickup tasks" for the next work block: At the end of each day or work unit, or before a significant pause or break, take a moment to generate a short list of small, easy tasks known as "pickup tasks" for the next day. You can also consciously choose something that you're quite excited about or personally find very enjoyable. Consider this a little "pre-reward" for getting over that initial hump required to restart any task.

Use a "parking lot" journal: We will cover this approach in a later section, but keep a written log of any thoughts and ideas that occur to you outside of your work block so that you can return to them instantly the next time you're scheduled to focus on that activity. "Park" random thoughts and ideas here and you've instantly identified something to pick up on next time.

Another thing to bear in mind is that as you cycle through these stages, you should do your absolute best to keep them completely clean and distinct. When you are working, do nothing but work. When you are resting, do nothing but rest. The entire system falls apart if you're muddling through your work with half a brain or thinking about all the things you're going to do while you're supposed to be relaxing. It's a great idea to literally and physically move yourself away from your work during your break times. Get up, leave your office or workstation, go outside, stretch, or do whatever you can to change the scenery.

Finally, be mindful about what is genuinely relaxing and restorative, and what is merely addictive or compulsive behavior. Scrolling social media, for example, can feel like a treat or relaxing activity, but often only stresses and tires you out further. If your work takes place on screens, spend your breaks away from screens; if your work is mostly seated, spend your breaks walking or napping; if your work is mostly done alone, spend your breaks connecting socially. You get the idea!

The Four Quarters Method

Using the 52:17 method, you take care of the hours and minutes of your schedule.

Now let's look at the days.

The four quarters method is a productivity technique that encourages viewing the day not as a single unit, but as four distinct starts, allowing for a fresh beginning if any particular quarter doesn't go well. This approach draws parallels with sports, where breaks or quarters offer teams opportunities to regroup and change the course of the game. Similarly, if a segment of your day doesn't go as planned, the method provides three more chances to reset and be productive.

While this is strictly a time management trick, it also has a lot to do with mindset management. A day is a natural unit of measurement, but sometimes if we "woke up on the wrong side of the bed," we can write off a day that could otherwise still be redeemed.

Realizing that the day actually contains many opportunities to start anew fosters motivation and control—and can help you get a lot more done. By reflecting on accomplishments throughout the day using the quarters system, you can learn to recognize your achievements, even if they are small. Breaking tasks into smaller chunks over multiple quarters makes the work seem more manageable, but it also creates four distinct moments for you to stop, reappraise, and give yourself a little reward—this is an incredible way of building motivation and momentum.

The way you divide your day will depend on your waking and sleeping times, but a good general guide is:

- Morning: around 5 a.m. to 9 a.m.
- Late Morning: around 10 a.m. to 1 p.m.
- Afternoon: around 2 p.m. to 7 p.m.
- Evening: around 7 p.m. onward

What's important is that you're dividing your day in a way that feels natural and meaningful to you—they don't have to be exactly the same length. For some people, structuring these blocks around meals makes sense; for others it's easier to work around major tasks such as leaving for work or coming home again.

Once you've decided on the four quarters, choose what your distinct **intention** is for each one.

For example:

- Morning: Prepare
- Late Morning: Produce
- Afternoon: Polish
- Evening: Unwind

Note that these are not tasks, but more like an overarching focus for the entire quarter. You'll notice that this will probably be inspired by your own natural biological rhythms—we'll talk more about optimizing in this way in a later chapter. Most people find they are best able to do their most difficult work in the morning or late morning, while the second two quarters are better used for planning, reflection, refining, consolidation, or rest.

Contain chaos in the late morning quarter by focusing on substantive work with minimal interruptions. Regroup in the afternoon quarter, adjusting priorities based on the day's developments. Rest and recover in the evening quarter by transitioning focus from output to renewal. This way, you're setting up a flow, with activities blending naturally from one to the next.

The morning can be thought of as the natural time to put your best foot forward and "start as you mean to continue." Unless you're a very unusual night-owl-type person or you do odd hours, morning quarter activities tend to include:

- Exercise
- Healthy habits
- Grooming, tidying chores, getting ready
- Journaling
- Meditation

- Reviewing schedules and goals, reordering priorities
- Quickly dispatching urgent tasks
- Making to-do lists and getting organized

Of course, most of us know what it's like to bungle through a bad morning—maybe a minor disaster derails our breakfast plans, we oversleep, or it's just a cold, rainy Monday morning and we don't exactly feel bright and shiny.

This is where the magic of the four quarters comes in, though. If a segment gets derailed, you can simply refocus on a fresh start in the next quarter. The system prevents a single setback from defining the entire day, offering regular checkpoints to get back on course.

Here's an example in action:

Georgia adopts the four-quarter method to improve her time management skills. Here is how a sample day unfolds:

Morning quarter (6 a.m.–9 a.m.):

Jen wakes up early to go for a run around the neighborhood and drink a healthy smoothie for breakfast. She sits down with a journal to reflect on the day ahead and sometimes finishes with meditation and visualization to get her in the right headspace. Finally, before tackling the day properly, she sets aside some time to answer any urgent emails, but the bulk of her workday doesn't start until the next quarter.

Late morning (9:30 a.m.–1 p.m.):

Jen blocks off this quarter for putting in the hours toward a big project that's due next week. She finds a nice quiet spot in a cafe and spends her second quarter doing deep, focused work on the most challenging parts of the project. She finishes this quarter by having lunch, recouping, and catching her breath for the next quarter.

Afternoon (2 p.m.–5:30 p.m.):

When Jen returns to the office, she's pretty tired. Rather than forcing herself to keep on with the project, she chooses instead to use the afternoon for less intense work, like meetings with colleagues, admin tasks and other chores that do not require her maximum brainpower. That aside, she is still using the afternoon's activities to feed back into the next day's morning quarter—for example, by keeping a notebook of interesting insights and avenues to explore when she next sits down with the project.

Evening (6 p.m.–9:30 p.m.):

Jen goes home after work and, since it's her turn to make dinner for her roommates, enjoys herself putting together the evening meal and relaxing with some conversation and TV. She calls her sister for a quick catch-up and finishes off her day with all the relaxing, pleasurable activities she loves best: reading in the bath, doing some gentle yoga, and tinkering with a few craft projects and hobbies.

Sounds great, doesn't it? But one day, if Georgia wakes up and feels a little off because she has a cold, she might not make her morning run, and when it comes time to journaling and meditating, her mind is all over the place, and she catches herself forgoing the healthy smoothie for something far less healthy. Those urgent emails are rushed off but could have been handled better.

Now what? By the time 10 a.m. rolls around, Georgia is into the next quarter. If she is still hung up and feeling guilty about her bad breakfast or skipping exercise, however, she may actually carry those negative feelings with her, causing her to be unfocused at the café and far less effective as she works on her project. The knock-on effects may last through the next two quarters as well, leaving her strung out and annoyed by 9 p.m., unable to unwind properly and stressed about the next day.

If she embraces the four quarters method, however, she realizes she doesn't have to waste mental energy dwelling on setbacks. Each quarter offers a fresh start—if you consciously and purposefully wipe that slate clean and refuse to let the previous few hours define the next few.

You might like to coincide your breaks with periods where you transition from one quarter to the next. If it works for you, try having a five-minute mindfulness session where you visualize yourself letting go of everything that came before, while at the same time preparing yourself to focus on the next task with fresh eyes and an open mind.

Every new quarter is also an opportunity to reassess goals and shift things around. Some people, for example, write themselves a to-do list at the start of the day and find it *psychologically impossible* to deviate from that list. Even if something serious comes up or doesn't go to plan, they feel like they've failed for not following through. But this all-or-nothing thinking is what undermines productivity—minor slipups only derail a day when we allow them to. Instead, double-check whether you may have been a little too ambitious or if a deadline needs to wiggle a little. People who are able to adjust and adapt in real time tend to get more done and feel better about doing it than those who cling to what "should" happen and then are unable to find a creative way through when it doesn't happen that way.

If chaos strikes and you find yourself dealing with a bad day, mentally remind yourself that it only has to go on until the next quarter. The emergency or chaos may still continue, but you can change the way you are responding to it, and you can choose how much you're willing to keep on engaging with it, and how. For example, if you're a parent who has a rotten morning trying to get the kids dressed and ready for school (every parent will recognize that feeling!), then help yourself cope by remembering that even the worst morning does not necessarily have to carry over. If we're honest with ourselves, sometimes the only reason we have a bad *day* is because we've consciously chosen to allow a bad *morning* to matter more than it needs to. Take a deep breath and move on. What is the intention you set for your next quarter? Focus on that because that's the only thing you can actually change.

The Twelve-Week Year Plan

The same idea that makes the four quarters method work so well can be applied to longer time periods too.

The concept of *The 12-Week Year* was introduced by authors Brian P. Moran and Michael Lennington, and it's all about challenging the habitual assumptions and behaviors we have around the concept of the classic yearlong plan. Just as a day is a natural unit of measurement, so is a year, with its inbuilt seasonal cycle. Just because these time frames are naturally occurring and convenient to use, however, it doesn't mean that they're *psychologically* the most productive way to think about and manage our time.

Moran and Lennington argue that a shorter, more focused approach leads to increased productivity and goal attainment. Their book, *The 12-Week Year: Get More Done in 12 Weeks than Others Do in 12 Months*, outlines a system to achieve peak performance by restructuring the annual timeline into four twelve-week cycles. Again, this is not really a time management shift, but a mindset shift.

Consider this example. You diligently set yourself some goals for the year in early January. You take a look at all the things you have planned to do in, say, August, and think, "That's ages away. I have plenty of time." And you do have plenty of time. But the effect of this "annualized thinking" is that by convincing you that you have endless time to do this, you also convince yourself to actually take that long. In other words, by putting your deadline in August, you are essentially preventing yourself from doing it before then. Not only that, but when August rolls around and life gets in the way, meaning you fail to meet that deadline, you may very well be tempted to reschedule for the following month or six months . . . or even August the *next* year.

The authors contend that planning for a full year is problematic due to the unpredictability of events and the tendency for individuals to fall into assuming there is ample time to achieve goals. In contrast, the twelve-week year philosophy emphasizes a shorter execution cycle, which brings benefits such as increased predictability, greater focus, and improved goal structure. In the same way as the four-quarter day reminds you that you can always start fresh, the twelve-week "year" also keeps you focused on smaller, more pragmatic chunks of time, leaving you plenty of opportunity to try again, adjust, or drop goals if they aren't working.

The benefits of a twelve-week execution cycle include heightened predictability by reducing the impact of unforeseen events, increased focus due to the urgency of a shorter time frame, and improved structure for clearer, well-defined goals aligning day-to-day actions with long-term visions.

To use this system effectively, the authors recommend thinking of three core principles and five disciplines. The core principles—accountability, commitment, and greatness in the moment—are deemed trainable qualities essential for success with the twelve-week system. The five disciplines—vision, planning, process control, measurement, and intentional time use—form a roadmap guiding users through implementing the twelve-week execution system.

Before we look at how this all comes together, a note on some useful terminology:

Strategic blocks and buffer blocks—These are time management tools that make your workday more efficient. A strategic block lasts two to three hours and focuses on high-level strategic tasks free from distractions. These could involve mapping out a roadmap or planning a new strategy. On the other hand, buffer blocks last about thirty minutes and are used for unplanned, low-value activities like answering emails or taking phone calls.

Lead indicators—These are metrics you can directly influence. When outlining the tactics to reach your goals, you'll want to define them based on lead indicators. Tasks might include "reach out to ten potential users every week" or "spend an hour a day conducting customer interviews."

Lag indicators—These are outcome-based metrics that result from your actions. They measure goals like "increase revenue by fifteen percent" and set them at the beginning of your twelve-week plan. Lag indicators give you a snapshot of the results you aim to achieve.

Implementing the "twelve-week year" system involves the following five steps:

Step 1: Build your vision statement

Developing a vision statement is crucial for guiding your twelve-week plan. This is not just for big corporations or for professional goals! Even smaller and more modest goals can benefit from a clear, focused vision statement.

Start by defining your aspirational vision, outlining your ultimate desires. This sets the long-term direction (identifying your priorities also keeps you focused—more on that in the next chapter). For larger projects, create a three-year vision as a progressive step toward your aspirations. For smaller ones, use your discretion and pick a shorter time scale.

Finally, formulate a twelve-month vision that provides a focused framework for everything you'll be tackling in the upcoming year. The idea is to align your short-term goals with your overarching vision, ensuring clarity and coherence in your objectives. While this step can sometimes feel a little tedious, it actually saves you a lot of extra work and potential confusion later down the line.

Example: Let's say you're currently in terrible physical shape but have a lifelong dream to complete an Ironman Triathlon and get in the best shape of your life. Your vision statement is something like "My vision is to successfully complete an Ironman Triathlon happening in twelve months' time and feel the pride and accomplishment that comes with mastering my own physical strength and determination, no matter what."

Step 2: Create your twelve-week plan

Next, translate your vision into actionable goals that can be achieved within a twelve-week time frame. Make these goals specific, measurable, achievable, relevant, and time-bound (SMART). Each goal should have corresponding tactics—which are short-term, action-oriented tasks that contribute to the achievement of the twelve-week goal. This step ensures that your aspirations are broken down into manageable and measurable components. Again, this step takes time, and of course the plan you outline will be adjusted and amended as you go along.

These more moderate tasks, however, act as a practical bridge between your everyday habits and your big long-term goals.

Example: You sketch out some broad goals for the year, dividing some milestones across the twelve months. But then you focus on just the first three months and look more closely at what you need to get started with first. Let's say your strategy is to start with your weakest skill, swimming. You set a twelve-week swimming goal and start breaking down tasks to get you there—for example, swim ten laps, then swim fifteen laps, then twenty, etc.

Step 3: Model your week through planning and accountability

Implement a weekly planning strategy to execute tasks in line with your twelve-week goals. Allocate specific time blocks, differentiating between strategic and buffer blocks. For example, you may spend one intense session a week figuring out your overall plan for the rest of the week. This not only helps you keep focused on the very next task at hand, but it encourages you to stay accountable to yourself. Treat these time blocks as one hundred percent non-negotiable—everything else can be moved to accommodate them, no excuses.

It's also a good idea to schedule regular accountability sessions with a peer to keep you on track. During these sessions, review your performance metrics and make necessary adjustments to stay on course. These sessions are not obligations you should dread, but rather valuable opportunities that you can use to keep refining, keep improving, keep learning.

Example: With all your twelve-week swimming goals in place, you get a clear sense of the weekly habits you need to start implementing right away. This immediately makes the big goal seem smaller and more manageable. Every Sunday evening you plan your week ahead, and every day in that week you do a swimming session at the gym pool.

Step 4: Implement scorekeeping and performance metrics

Maintain a scorecard to track your actions and outcomes throughout the twelve weeks. This scorecard serves as a tool to measure your effectiveness and identify any areas for improvement, or on the other hand, identify what's working so you can do more of it. How you track and monitor your progress is up to you. You could include efficiency ratios, financial metrics, or engagement indicators, and analyze the data from both lag and lead indicators.

You could also make use of more qualitative dating and ratings to track more subtle indicators that you are improving. By following performance metrics closely, you gain insights into the actions needed to stay on track toward your goals. Naturally, the nature of your goal will determine the kind of tracking metric you need to use.

Example: You keep close track of the time it takes you to swim a lap, of your body weight and composition, of your diet and how many hours you're sleeping, and of how you're feeling generally. Maybe you notice that you perform worse during certain times of day, or that you're plateauing at a certain level. You keep tabs on all this and adjust accordingly.

Step 5: Review and reset

At the end of the twelve weeks, it is essential to pause, reflect, and regroup. Reflection of this kind is a strong point in the twelve-week framework. If you only conduct this kind of appraisal once a year, you're missing the chance to make course corrections earlier on. Do it four times a year and your goals may evolve much more quickly by being refined more regularly.

Conduct a thorough review of your outcomes, analyzing both successful and unsuccessful elements. This needs to be done in as neutral and non-judgmental a way as possible. Depending on your goal, there may be some difficult feelings to manage around expectations, failure, fear, and frustration. But your job at this stage is to acknowledge those feelings while not letting them interfere with your ability to clearly see what needs to be done. You are not condemning any failures or clinging to any lucky successes—you are simply looking at your plan, how well you implemented it, and what you might do better next time—no shame, judgment, or avoidance required.

Use the insights gained from this step to inform your next twelve-week cycle, allowing for continuous improvement and adaptability in your goal-setting and achievement process. One amazing way to deal with any uncomfortable emotions like fear, disappointment, frustration, and so on is to channel that energy directly back into another goal—a *better* goal. This ensures that you're never really wasting time overanalyzing and "processing" obstacles and missteps—your commitment to immediately take inspired action *is* how you process and move on.

Example: When the twelve-week chunk is over, you stop and review—you're surprised by how far you've come! Your fitness level is higher, and your needs and expectations are a little different now. You look at the provisional yearlong goal you made and realize that some tweaks are necessary. There are a few smaller goals you've failed to accomplish, but you work hard to understand why you didn't, and you commit to not making the same mistake for the next twelve-week period, where you start to tackle the cycling portion of the triathlon training.

The Pickle Jar Theory

So, by using the 52:17 method (keeping track of minutes and hours), the four quarters method (keeping track of the days), and the twelve-week year framework (keeping track of the weeks and months in a year), you are empowering yourself to better manage time in the short-, medium-, and long-term range.

At some point, however, you will come up against a non-negotiable truth about time: It's a finite resource, and nothing we can do will help us make more of it. We'll end this chapter on the "pickle jar theory," which is not a technique or method but rather a metaphor that helps us take a certain approach to time and time management.

Even if you're excellent at managing your time, it's inevitable that occasionally you'll find yourself running out of it or having to choose between two equally important tasks. The best of us can find ourselves feeling extremely busy, and yet somehow, we're not moving the needle when it comes to what really matters. The reason is usually a question not just of priorities but of understanding how tasks differ in their importance and urgency, and how to budget time and energy wisely.

Let me give you an intuitive example: I had a friend who was always busy. She was always doing something and always active, as though every minute of her day was spoken for. One day her and her partner decided to start trying for a baby, and I wondered where on earth she would find the time in her schedule to raise a child. She said, "We'll make time," and that's precisely what she seemed to do. When the baby came, her life accommodated the additional work, and she was just as busy as ever, yet still somehow never rushed or overwhelmed.

Today, my friend has *four* children, and I still look on and wonder how it all fits together. I used to chalk it up to some kind of magic or luck, but now I understand that my friend was actually using the "pickle jar" approach long before it had a name.

The theory was first introduced by Jeremy Wright in 2002, and he also called it the bucket of rocks theory. The central idea is that time is a non-perishable resource with limits, similar to the volume of a pickle jar or a bucket. It's a visual representation that suggests that just like the space in the jar or bucket, our time has real, non-negotiable limits.

To manage time effectively, then, it is crucial to assign priorities to tasks. In the pickle jar theory, tasks are categorized into sand, pebbles, rocks, and water, each representing different levels of importance and urgency. The rocks are the biggest, most important tasks and goals, with the pebbles and sand representing smaller and less important tasks.

First, imagine that someone takes an empty pickle jar and has to fit a quantity of sand, pebbles, rocks, and water into it. They try to do so by pouring in the water and the sand. Then they squash the pebbles on top of that mud, and finally try to pack in the big rocks. But there's a problem—it doesn't all fit. The rocks can't be squeezed in completely and so they have to be left out.

This situation is analogous to a life where you waste all your time on the little, insignificant tasks, and then have nothing left to devote to the tasks that really matter. You are "busy" all the time (i.e., your jar is legitimately full), but you are not getting any closer to reaching your main goals or working on your most valued priorities.

You could try again with a different strategy. First put in your big rocks and make sure that you are giving them priority in your pickle jar. Then take the pebbles you have—the tasks that are important but can be more flexibly added into your schedule around the bigger goals. Once they're in place, pour in the sand, which will easily flow into the tiny cracks and spaces between the bigger rocks and pebbles. Finally, take your water and pour it in—even with a jar that seems quite full, water has a knack of finding a place for itself. Now, you see that all the tasks that "didn't fit" before *do* fit.

This, I discovered, is the secret to my friend's approach. She always knew how to devote the bulk of her time and energy to what most mattered to her, and she allowed the smaller, less significant things to find their way into the spaces that remained. Actually, in my friend's case, it wasn't that her four children were the insignificant water that fitted into the rest of her work life; rather, she changed what she considered her big rocks—her priorities—to be. The amount of space in the jar was always the same, but *how* it fit together was never left to chance.

Now, this is just a metaphor. The idea is to emphasize that if you manage your time poorly, you will never seem to have enough of it, but if you manage it well, you can become so productive that it may start to look like magic! It also drives home the fact that we need to treat big tasks and goals differently to little ones. Little tasks and goals, by their nature, can be done here and there, in a few spare moments, and without too much effort. In a way, they can work themselves out in the day's leftover time.

The big goals, however, cannot be managed this way. Some goals are so big that you cannot squeeze them in if the jar is even half full. In other words, the *only* way you can get that task done is to put it first—if you don't, it will never get done. As an example, consider the big task of writing a novel. You may have a daily "rock" task of writing five thousand words for your novel—no mean feat. This goal is more important to you than anything else in your world right now, yet when you wake up in the morning, the first thing you do is waste an hour on social media. Then you fritter away more time on housework, emails, and a few other non-essential tasks. After lunch you sit down to tackle your five thousand words. You're now tired, however, and the task seems overwhelming. The day's already half gone, after all. You do the task partway or procrastinate the entire thing, thinking, "Why is there never enough time?!"

Instead, you could have woken up and dedicated the first few hours of the morning to getting those five thousand words done, no excuses. Then, all those pebble and sand tasks could be squeezed in later, after the big rock was firmly in place. Have you ever heard anyone complain that there's "never enough time" to look at social media or watch TV? Probably not! Unfortunately, we prioritize the low-value tasks and jeopardize the high-value ones.

In the traditional pickle jar theory, the water is conceptualized as time with family and friends, as well as your own health and well-being. Get the work done, the theory says, and you can have a life with what's left. This attitude may not fit if you're the kind of person who values and prioritizes your family, friends, and well-being, i.e., if those are in fact your big rocks.

Again, the theory is just a metaphor, so you can adjust it to fit your circumstances as needed. What matters is simple: The big and important tasks need to get first pick of your time and attention. Life always requires a little adjustment and renegotiation, but if you must compromise on something, make sure it's your less important goals and never your most important ones.

Summary:

- Julia Gifford has found that the most productive people tend to follow a cycle of working for fifty-two minutes and then taking a break for seventeen minutes. This approach can be combined with the classic Pomodoro Technique, which suggests a twenty-five-minute work period with five minutes' rest in between.
- The numbers are not what matters—what you do with them counts. When you plan your time effectively, less work can actually mean more work.
- The four-quarter method encourages you to divide the day up into defined quarters—morning, late-morning, afternoon, and evening—so that each new segment is a fresh opportunity to start again. Schedule

defined task categories for each window, e.g., always exercise in the first quarter.
- The twelve-week year plan helps you break down the year into more manageable, medium-term chunks in the same way. It emphasizes a shorter execution cycle, which brings benefits such as increased predictability, greater focus, and improved goal structure, plus more opportunities for course correction and adjustment.
- Finally, the pickle jar theory is an extended metaphor that helps explain how you can fit your tasks in order of their priority, given the finite amount of time you have each day. By placing your "rocks" into the jar *first* and then fitting in pebbles, sand, and water in the remaining space, you ensure everything fits and that you are never devoting time to insignificant tasks at the expense of your priorities.

Chapter 2: Take Control of Your Priorities/Focus

> *"The key is not to prioritize what's on your schedule, but to schedule your priorities."—Stephen Covey,* The 7 Habits of Highly Effective People

When you look at a weekly, monthly, or yearly calendar, you might get the impression that all those little blocks, all those days, are there and available for you to use. Maybe you look at all those little blocks and conclude that you have plenty of time available to work on your dreams and projects. The truth is, however, that you don't. All you have is those days that you *actively seize and dedicate* to the pursuit of those dreams—and every day that you fail to do this is another day that you don't "have."

The things that truly matter to us will never get done by accident. The plain truth is that nobody else is going to make our dreams their priority—

that's our job. We will never receive an invitation to do better, we will never feel one hundred percent ready to start, and we don't need to ask for or earn permission to value what we value. If you want to achieve something in the future, then what you do today, right now, matters. This is what our second chapter is about: getting crystal clear on what we want to focus on and what we don't.

Anti-Overcommitment Formula

Many people mistakenly identify their problem as a lack of productivity, when in reality their issues stem from overcommitment.

In the previous section we saw that even though time management is essential, it also matters how you prioritize tasks and what goes into the jar first, so to speak. You can see the problem of overcommitment in a similar way: When you only have rocks to fit in your jar, sooner or later you're going to find that nothing fits.

Let's say you're someone who's seriously trying to work on your personal development, and that means improving your health, your relationships, your career, your home life, and your finances. You're motivated to do all these things, and they are important. The problem is, you don't have enough room in your jar for that many big rocks. You need to prioritize. Not being able to successfully fit in several major life goals at once does *not* mean that you are bad at time management or that you need to find ways to be more productive. There is no productivity hack on earth that will make all those rocks fit.

Too often, people embark on self-improvement missions and attempt to do too much at once. They make several changes to their lifestyles, set themselves multiple ambitious goals across many different areas of life, and then get frustrated when they don't seem able to muster enough time/energy to get everything done. Rather than reappraise their expectations, they wonder what they can do to become more "productive."

The pressure of excessive commitments leads to a sense of time debt. Sometimes those are commitments that are placed on us by outside forces, but if we're honest, we are often the ones placing at least some of this pressure on ourselves. Managing expectations is key; modest goals worked on consistently may not seem as glamorous as dramatic overnight success stories, but the irony is that a more measured approach almost always leads to better outcomes in the long run.

Elizabeth Grace Saunders is a time management coach who has suggested a handy formula to help you explore this issue objectively. She says, "The single most important factor in feeling like a time investment success or failure is whether or not your expectations of what you will accomplish align with how much time you have to invest."

Her formula is a way to mathematically understand the relationship between your expectations and the limited amount of time you have to budget toward those expectations. Once you can see this relationship in black and white, you can make smart adjustments so that you're always "finding time" for what matters most. You'll have been told time and time again to "focus on your priorities," but what's great about Saunders's formula is that you can start to put numbers on what that actually means.

The formula goes like this:

(External Expectations) + (Internal Expectations) ≤ 24 hours – (Self-Care)

Let's take a look at how to use it.

Step 1: Calculate your self-care number by finding the self-care categories you need for your well-being, and totaling the hours you spend.

For example:

- Sleeping—8 hours
- Meals and meal prep—1 hour
- Grooming—1 hour

Add up the time values for each category to find your self-care number:

Self-Care Number = Sleeping + Meals + Grooming

The total is 10 hours.

Step 2: Assess total commitments

List and categorize your external expectations (e.g., work, commute, family, pets, relationships, community obligations) and internal expectations (e.g., hobbies, side projects, personal time). And then calculate the total hours.

For example:

- External Expectations:
    - 8 for work + 1 for housework + 1 for family time = 10 hours
- Internal Expectations:
    - 1 for games and TV + 1 for reading + 1 for side projects = 3 hours

Total internal and external commitments is therefore 13 hours.

Step 3: Use the equation and substitute its values

Plug your values into the equation:

(External Expectations) + (Internal Expectations) ≤ 24 hours − (Self-Care)

13 ≤ 24 hours − (8 for sleep + 1 for eating + 1 for grooming)

13 ≤ 24 hours − 10

13 ≤ 14

Step 4: Evaluate the result

After adding both sides, take a look at the overall "equation." Is the left side of your equation less than or equal to the right side? If the left side exceeds the right, it means you are overcommitted, risking burnout. In our above example, you're working pretty optimally and even have an hour of wiggle room, which is ideal.

What to Do with Your Results

If the left side of your equation is very much greater than the right.

You are likely overcommitted. It's time to take a look at your expectations and the demands currently on you. Are most of them coming from you or from others (i.e., internal or external)? It may be that a demand you characterize as external is actually internal—once you realize this, you're at liberty to decide if you want to drop it. If there are too many external demands, it's a sign you need to tighten up your boundaries and say *no* more, or else postpone some goals or tasks for later.

If the left side of your equation is just a little greater than the right.

You're doing well but you may have a tendency to attempt too much. Do you have a few commitments that you are devoting too much time to? In this case, it may be that certain productivity hacks and more discipline will help. Take a look at where your hours are going and see if you can identify any less-significant "sand" or "pebble" tasks—you may need to bump these down the list of priorities or simply devote less time to them overall.

If the right side is very much greater than the right side.

There could be one of two big problems here. The first is that the left side is too low, i.e., you are not applying yourself to your full potential. Double-check that you are accurately counting up the demands and expectations you have of yourself and that others have of you, and, if this is genuinely less than the total hours you have in a day, this is good news: you have room to grow.

The other problem may be more serious, and comes from the right side of the equation, i.e., you are not allocating enough time for self-care (that or you are living in a universe with fewer than twenty-four hours in a day!). Look closely and see where you might be short-changing yourself. Do you need more sleep, more relaxation, more quality time with people you love?

If the right side is just a little greater than the left side.

This may be the ideal ratio to aim for. Being a tiny bit under committed gives you the flexibility to respond to changes and adjust day to day. You don't want to be tightly scheduled right down to the minute so that every little problem throws you off course. An extra thirty minutes or hour in a day can act like oil in the engine of your life, and this little bit of "give" in your schedule can help everything else run more smoothly.

One final thing to consider is the ratio between your external and internal expectations. There's been plenty of ink spilled about work-life balance, but it's not so simple as weighing up the one against the other. There are different kinds of work—paid work, work in the home, work we do on our own side projects or hobbies, raising kids, etc. A person with a family, a job, and a relationship will likely have more external demands and obligations than a single student. Nobody can tell you what the ideal ratio is, but carefully consider your own values and examine whether this is reflected in the way you're actually spending your time day to day.

For example, if you value your family and say that they are your priority, then it doesn't quite make sense to devote a mere thirty minutes to them a day, while you blow five hours on TV and mindless scrolling. At the same time, if you are serious about a goal to, say, launch your own business, your time budget should reflect that priority—self-care is great, but it doesn't make sense to cancel your networking event to attend a three-hour meditation class instead.

Build a Parking Lot

When left to its own devices, life tends to get chaotic and messy. The moment you devote yourself to a single, uninterrupted task, you are likely to find a host of distractions emerging to divert your attention. Having traits of ADD or ADHD can make the problem even worse, and your mind may constantly come up with additional unrelated ideas. You may be working on an email but then suddenly switch tabs so you can double-check on a shopping cart you have elsewhere at an online store. Before checking out and completing the sale, you suddenly start thinking about what's happening tomorrow, and quickly check your calendar. Then you're thinking about dinner. Then you're back to the shopping cart.

We've all experienced this kind of scattiness before, but *why* does it happen?

One theory is that your brain is, in its own way, trying to help you. Our attention evolved in an environment far less stimulating than the modern world, and our ability to quickly switch focus and pay attention to something new was an important adaptation that helped us survive. When you self-distract with a "pop-up thought," you are doing much the same thing, and your brain quickly focuses on the new thing just in case it's important. You may get a strong feeling that you need to act on this impulse to switch attention, because if you don't, you may forget or miss a crucial opportunity.

When you eventually return to the original task, you might forget where you left off, skip steps, or waste time refocusing. Not only are you being less efficient, but you're also stressing yourself out—it's a lose-lose.

Now, if this phenomenon happens because we have a kind of "ideational FOMO" (fear of missing out), then one way to tackle it is to make sure our brains know that we are *not* going to miss out on an opportunity, that we *won't* forget an important piece of information, and that we do *not* have to act immediately on every impulse.

We can do this by building a so-called mental parking lot.

This is simply a place where you can quickly jot down any fleeting thoughts so you can return to what you were doing without worrying about forgetting anything important. Essentially, when you put something in your parking lot, you are telling your brain, "Don't worry, it's all taken care of. Just focus on what you're doing right now, and you can think about everything else later, when it's the right time."

The idea is that whatever distracting daydream, worry, memory, or idea pops into your mind, you can effectively say to it, "Not right now," and release any anxiety about losing track of it or forgetting. People who are frequently distracted do not have objectively busier or more chaotic lives; rather, they have an impaired ability to quickly sort through incoming mental stimuli and recognize which ones require a complete shift of attention and which are insignificant and can be disregarded or "parked" for later. The parking lot technique can in time teach you to be more focused and aware of this very process so that you internalize the idea that just because a thought pops into your head, it doesn't mean you *have to* follow it, and it certainly doesn't mean you have to follow it right now!

Create a Two-Part Habit

Part 1: Park your information

The parking lot can be a digital space (phone's Notes, Evernote, Google Docs) or a literal notebook you keep nearby (some people like to use one with a colorful, eye-catching cover). Any time you notice your attention has been suddenly hooked by sudden thoughts, ideas, directions, questions, or things like emails, notifications, and messages, stop and briefly write it down in the parking lot. For example, let's say you're busy writing a long and complicated email when you suddenly have an intrusive thought: "Oops! Did I remember to add a secondary driver to that car rental I arranged for the weekend? Is that something I even have to do?" You notice that you are completely engrossed in this idea and no longer focused on the email. Instead of opening a new tab and looking into this new idea, get out your parking lot notebook and scribble something like: *secondary driver for car rental?* Then close the book, mentally tell yourself that you will investigate this thought later, when you're done with your current task, and carry on.

Part 2: Parking lot review for action

Just keeping a parking lot on its own is meaningless. You'll need to also develop a daily ritual to review everything you've put in there! You might like to tie the review to existing routines like planning or email checking, that way it fits in seamlessly with your existing habits and won't be overlooked. Dedicate a *fixed* amount of time to reviewing this notebook—it's important that you keep this window defined and limited.

Let's say the following morning you look in your parking lot and see the item *secondary driver for car rental?* You think about how to transform this into an actionable item. It may be that you need to write something in a calendar, put it on a to-do list, break it down further into smaller chunks and assign yourself milestones for those chunks, or even delegate/ignore entirely.

Putting up Your Boundaries

Some of us are our own worst enemies, and in truth we are the ones who are continually derailing ourselves. Sometimes, though, it's other people who are undermining our efforts. For example:

- You did a favor for someone at work once and now they just expect you to keep doing it, and so you spend ten minutes of every day doing it even when you're extremely busy.
- You're in your office or study and just settling down to some deep work when someone comes knocking at the door . . . and they come knocking again ten minutes later, and a third time before the hour is up.
- You have a pushy client who emails you late on a Sunday night, demanding updates and explanations, so you sit in bed on your phone, groggily typing out a response.

The unreasonable demands that other people place on us also belong in the parking lot. We can use the parking lot for anything that threatens to flow into a space that we have planned and dedicated to some other purpose. In other words, the parking lot concept is really all about boundaries.

The thing is, just like irritating device notifications and junk mail, other people's demands and interruptions *will* happen—and it's not personal. Rather, it's up to us to put firm barriers and limits in place. People won't know or care that they're encroaching on you unless you are aware that they are, and are clearly communicating that with them!

A good boundary is one that is reasonable, clearly communicated, polite, and (most important) comes with built-in natural consequences. Think carefully about what is intruding into your focused work time, your energy, or your attention, and make sure that you are clearly and politely communicating this to others. Then, when people press on or overstep that boundary, you need to be ready to easily follow through with a natural consequence.

You ask your colleague to do the job themselves or find another person to help them. You do the job just once more and never again; if this puts them in a difficult spot, that's their problem and not yours. You put a polite DO NOT DISTURB notice on your door, and if people keep walking in, you lock the door. You explain clearly to the client when you are and aren't available, and if they continue to make trouble, you terminate that relationship.

Setting and asserting boundaries is not always easy, but it's usually easier than trying to live with weak, ineffectual, or confusing boundaries. Recognize that boundaries and limits are things that add value to life—yours and others. Saying no to some things is what allows you to say yes to others.

The Worry Journal

Some therapists use a version of the parking lot called a "worry journal," and it works the same way. The great thing about putting worries and ruminations into a journal is that when you eventually do get around to processing them, enough time might have passed that you realize you are no longer concerned about it. This is excellent training for avoiding overthinking, because you learn to acknowledge worries without engaging with them. You may see that much of what grabs your attention in the moment is not actually urgent or important; it just feels that way. If left alone, many negative feelings often pass on their own, and issues resolve themselves.

A word of warning, however: you don't want to get too distracted by the act of writing in the journal itself. Simply make a few notes (just one or two words will do) and then quickly move on. You need to consciously tell yourself that you are no longer worrying about this issue. It's natural that your brain will keep popping up little mental "notifications" as though it were saying, "What about this thing, though? Shouldn't we be worried about it? Are you sure we shouldn't be focused on that right now?" This is normal, but it will get better with practice.

Notice the impulse, and notice yourself ignoring it.

Day Theming

One excellent (and pretty obvious) way of taking control of your priorities is with day theming—which is exactly what it sounds like. All you need to do is assign each day a broad category or theme and commit to prioritizing those tasks and activities that match that theme. The value of this approach is not that it makes you more productive, so to speak. What it does do is stop you from creating too many opportunities where you *lose* productivity, i.e., every time you switch tasks.

Imagine that you've started off your morning working well on a tricky project. You're halfway through it when you're suddenly summoned to a last-minute meeting that wasn't supposed to happen until next week. You go to the meeting, but because it's so last minute, everyone takes a while to focus and get to business. By the time the meeting is finished, you're late starting up some other commitment you planned for that afternoon, and then spend the first fifteen minutes of that window trying to catch your breath and figure out what you're trying to do.

Every time you switch tasks, you unsettle your brain and lose momentum. Settling again takes time and effort. In fact, psychologist David Meyer claims that shifting tasks can eat up forty percent of your productive time. The more task switching you do, the more time needs to go to admin, travel, settling in, figuring out where you left off, booting up computers, starting software, getting comfortable, and most importantly, getting yourself in the right headspace to work.

Try to imagine that every task switch comes with a price—a price you pay in productivity. Flip-flopping from task to task not only lowers the quality of your work and makes mistakes more likely, but it also stresses you out, impairs your memory, and keeps you from entering that deep work "flow" state where you are best able to solve problems well and think creatively. So, while you may be tempted to draw up a complicated schedule where you squeeze in a wide variety of tasks done in hour chunks, be aware that it may not be as efficient as it looks— the head and tail of each of those hour chunks may actually be lost in the shuffle!

The goal with day theming, then, is to switch tasks as little as possible—preferably not at all. Set the intention to spend the bulk of your effort and awareness on one thing at a time. Priorities are not just something you "have." A priority should be thought of as something you **do**. It is a commitment to continually choose the place your attention goes, and to sustain that attention in one direction. This takes discipline, but it also builds discipline the more practice you get. If you can continually keep distractions at bay, you will strengthen your ability to focus for longer periods and with more depth.

Here's how to start incorporating day theming into your life:

1. Decide on core categories

Identify the major areas of your life that consistently demand time and attention—i.e., your priorities and those tasks that lead directly to the accomplishment of your goals and ambitions. These are those categories of activity that require the most from you, whether that's deep work, creativity, or sustained focus for long periods. You may end up with seven different themes for seven different days in the week, or you may find you only have two or three themes and cycle through them as needed.

If you're a student, for example, your categories might include classes, study sessions, personal projects, and relaxation. If you're working on marketing your business, you may choose categories like meetings, correspondence, research, or content creation. Don't worry if this step feels a little vague initially. You can always adjust as you go along.

2. Assign themes to specific days

Next, make sure you're allocating enough time to each category, bearing in mind the importance of work-life balance. Remember the overcommitment formula and make sure that you're not overcommitting yourself while leaving no room for self-care, home maintenance, family life, health, and so on.

For example, if you're a training athlete, you may decide that you want to dedicate Monday to cardio exercise, Tuesday to flexibility, Wednesday to strength, and so on. You may pick Sunday as the family and friends day, and Saturday for non-sports-related hobbies and activities.

3. Write out specific tasks

List out all the tasks, small or large, related to each theme. Categorize these tasks into daily, weekly, monthly, quarterly, and yearly, and keep updating the list as new tasks arise and old tasks are achieved. This step is pretty much identical to what you'd be doing in the "twelve-week year" plan.

For an example, you might be embarking on a complex home renovation project that requires months of coordinated action on all sorts of tasks. You may need to spend some time creating a folder where you break these tasks down into themed days, and then break those tasks down further so that you know what you're doing minute by minute, and hour by hour, in that day. Let's say you decide that

Thursday is going to be a painting day, and then break down that job into prep work, painting in the edges and corners, doing the main part of the walls, second coats, and tidying up. Depending on the complexity of the task, you can keep breaking things down further and further.

4. Add themes and tasks to your calendar

One final step is to schedule your themes and specific tasks on your calendar. There is an element here of commitment and determination—you need to feel that once you've committed to tackling a certain theme on a certain day, then nothing will stop you. Of course, that doesn't mean that you can't observe, evaluate, and adjust as you go along. It's par for the course that you make some tweaks as you go. For example, you may devote Fridays to learning vocabulary in your new chosen language, but discover after a few weeks that Friday is your least productive day, and vocabulary your most difficult task. After observing your performance and energy levels, you decide to switch to Monday or Tuesday when you're feeling more refreshed.

What about Emergencies?

Now, you're probably thinking that this all sounds great, but what happens if there's a genuine emergency that you cannot avoid? Well, there is just no way to avoid the unavoidable or predict the unpredictable. If you're cultivating focus and priorities with day theming, however, you may find that removing unnecessary distractions actually make you more available to respond flexibly when there is a genuine crisis.

Using what we've already learned from the four quarters method of day planning, we can make sure that a crisis in the middle of the day doesn't have to derail the entire day. If a twenty-minute emergency crops up during a one-hour task session, it's far harder to recover than if the emergency occurs during a full day of focusing on that task, where the twenty minutes only represents a small distraction in context.

This is also the place where your wiggle room comes in handy (recall the anti-overcommitment equation) and where an extra hour here and there can give you the flexibility you need to catch up on interrupted tasks later on, without losing any headway. Finally, remember that you often have way more power and control in your ability to *interpret* events than you usually think. Ask yourself whether something demanding your attention truly is an emergency in the first place. Remember that "failure to plan on your part does not constitute an emergency on my part."

People make mistakes, things come up, and plans don't always, well, go to plan. It's great to be kind, forgiving, and accommodating of people. That said, you can meet other people's demands without allowing them to dictate the speed and urgency with which you do so. You can be compassionate *and* maintain your boundaries. For example, "I'm so sorry to hear that. I'd be happy to help you fix things up. I'm busy right now, but I'm available tomorrow evening if you want to sit down together and work something out?"

How to Bubble Sort

When it comes to priorities, you already know that you're supposed to consistently focus on the things that are most important. But how can you do that when *everything* feels like it's super important?

This problem is most evident when it comes to to-do lists. If you've carefully identified the week's and the day's tasks and scheduled everything you're supposed to do, how do you know where to start?

Bubble Sort is a simple sorting algorithm that works by repeatedly stepping through your to-do list, comparing adjacent elements, and swapping them if they are in the wrong order. It is called "bubble sort" because smaller elements gradually "bubble" to the top of the list while larger elements "sink" to the bottom.

The bubble sort method, traditionally used in computer science for sorting elements in an array, can be adapted for task prioritization and the management of an intimidating to-do list. Instead of sorting numbers or data, you'll be sorting tasks based on their relative importance. Let's break down the steps and the rationale behind using this method:

1. Lay out your tasks in vertical columns.
2. Take a look at the top/first two on your list and compare them. Considering only

these two, which one should have priority over the other? Arrange them to reflect your ranking.
3. Now move down to consider the next pair of columns. Repeat your comparison and move the tasks accordingly so that the most important tasks are gradually "bubbling" to the top.
4. Read through the entire list again to make sure you're happy with the order, and then you can start completing the tasks.

Bubble sorting is extremely simple, but it won't work unless you're crystal clear on the criteria by which you're comparing and ranking each item. Just remember that you're always looking for relative importance. Here, "important" means that a task is something that directly leads to the accomplishment of your priority goals, or otherwise would cause significant problems were it not completed. For example, if preparing for an exam is this week's big priority, then tasks like revising your notes and completing practice papers count as important tasks. Of course, you may also have the task "pay parking fine before they double it," and this definitely counts as important, even though it doesn't relate to your goals or priorities.

Be careful that you are not inadvertently ranking items lower in importance than you should because these tasks are unpleasant and you'd rather avoid them. Think about Mark Twain and his frog quote: "If it's your job to eat a frog, it's best to do it first thing in the morning. And if it's your job to eat two frogs, it's best to eat the biggest one first." Keeping this in mind, it may even make sense to ask yourself to rank tasks specifically according to how much you're dreading them and how likely you are to be tempted to procrastinate doing them.

Let's look at exactly how you could use a bubble sort on a to-do list.

Step 1: Set up the grid

Tasks are initially assigned to unique cells in a horizontal grid. This creates a visual representation of the tasks. Of course, you can lay out your list vertically if you want, but this way around makes it a little easier to visualize.

| Task 1 | Task 2 | Task 3 | Task 4 | Task 5 | Task 6 |

Step 2: Compare the first two tasks

Now begin by comparing the importance of two adjacent tasks. This comparison is done by asking, "Which task is more important?" This is a subjective evaluation based on your criteria for importance, so you do need to be honest and realistic.

For example, your first two tasks may be "Task 1: Organize bank statements for business account" and "Task 2: Complete application form for grant." On the face of it, it may not seem easy to choose between some tasks, but you can get a good idea of their importance by asking what would happen if you didn't do the task and how long those consequences will take to appear. Also ask which one is more difficult. You may decide that completing the application forms takes more time and is trickier and cannot be avoided, whereas organizing bank statements has no real deadline and can even be delegated to someone other than you.

| Task 1 | Task 2 | Task 3 | Task 4 | Task 5 | Task 6 |

Step 3: Reorder the tasks

In this case, Task 2 (the application form) was more important than Task 1 (the bank statements), so you switch them around. Now, you keep going in this way, but your next comparison happens between the next two columns. At this point, Task 1 and Task 3 are in these positions, and so you compare them against one another.

Task 1 is still the bank statements, and Task 3 may be "notify registration board of change of address." You decide that Task 1 is actually a little more important than Task 3, so you leave them as they are. Then you move down and compare the tasks in the third and fourth row, continuing to compare and reorder until you get to the end of the tasks. As you go, more important tasks shift to the left, and less important ones to the right.

| Task 2 | Task 1 | Task 3 | Task 4 | Task 5 | Task 6 |

5. Final Prioritization

You want to make sure that your final ordering genuinely reflects the order of each task's importance, so each one is more important than the one to its right, and less important than the one to its left. This is an iterative process, so you may need to go through the list again, from the beginning, a few times. You may end up with a list that looks very different from what you started with.

| Task 2 | Task 1 | Task 6 | Task 4 | Task 3 | Task 5 |

A few notes about this process:

- It will work best for longer lists where it is not immediately clear where to start. You can use the process for short lists, too, but you may only need to do this mentally and juggle the order without formally setting things up in columns.

- When you're finished, one thing to do is to look at the tasks right at the bottom of the list. Do you even need to do them at all? You might like to delegate or just eliminate this task entirely. Another possibility is to fold this task into another, more important one.
- If the tasks at the end of the list are very small and take only five to ten minutes to do, it may be more efficient to just do them at once, rather than waste any more time processing and organizing them on a list. If you can fire off an email in two minutes, for example, just do it the very second it comes into your inbox.
- You can apply this process to a list that contains mixed items, but it works best if you are day theming and sorting tasks that all relate to the same general category or activity. This is because it can be difficult to compare and rank items meaningfully if they're from different areas of life.

Avoid the Urgency Trap

Sorting your tasks based on their importance is a great skill to learn. Bubble sorting continually pushes you to rate *relative* importance, driving home the fact that not everything can be important. If the nature of your work and tasks means you're struggling to get a handle on what's important and what isn't, you might like to use what's called the Eisenhower Principle. The concept is named after former US president Dwight D. Eisenhower and a speech he gave in 1954, but the original quote actually comes from Dr. J. Roscoe Miller, the then-president of Northwestern University. The quote goes,

"I have two kinds of problems: the urgent and the important. The urgent are not important, and the important are never urgent." This quote has since become the foundation of an approach for planning and prioritizing tasks.

Many of us don't quite understand the difference between important and urgent.

Important activities are those that link us in a meaningful way to our goals and the things we ultimately value.

Urgent activities are those that are time sensitive—they are the kind of things that we usually do in order to avoid some undesirable consequence later on. These things often have more to do with other people's goals and values than they do with ours!

We can put these two dimensions into a matrix and create four possible categories of problems:

- Unimportant and not urgent

- Unimportant and urgent
- Important and not urgent
- Important and urgent

The order the tasks are listed in above is in order of ascending importance. For tasks that are unimportant and not urgent, our approach is obvious: Ignore or avoid them entirely.

For tasks that are unimportant and urgent, find a way to dispatch them as quickly as possible, perhaps automating the things you absolutely cannot avoid. You may also need to have careful boundaries to say no to other people's demands that don't actually concern you.

For tasks that are important and not urgent, take care to consistently block off time in your schedule. These are the things that matter a lot in the grand scheme, but which will never constitute an emergency, so do your best to develop discipline here and put in the hours even though you could easily get away with not doing so.

For tasks that are important and urgent, do these first and dedicate your best resources to their completion.

Combining the Eisenhower Principle with bubble sorting, you can see that asking whether a task is both important and urgent can help you more effectively rank and prioritize. Whatever you do, don't waste time on tasks that don't matter and aren't urgent, and if you are choosing between two equally important tasks, do the one that is most urgent first. It's up to *you* to decide what counts as urgent, however, because these rankings are relative to your own goals, your own values, and everything else you currently have on your list.

Summary:

- When you take control of your priorities, you are consciously choosing what you value and where you want to spend your effort, attention, and energy. Often, procrastination and lack of productivity is actually because we're overcommitted and fracturing our focus. Elizabeth Grace Saunders's "anti-overcommitment formula" is a tool to help you strategically measure where you're spending yourself, and make adjustments according to what you most value.
- Distractions, diversions, and interruptions are an inevitable part of life. But we don't have to respond to them. If you're in the middle of focused work, use a "parking lot" journal to note down intrusive thoughts and return to them later—if at all. This method can also be used to manage overthinking and rumination.

- Day theming is a way to stay focused and involves assigning each day a broad category or theme and committing to prioritizing those tasks and activities that match that theme. This allows you to cut down on that little loss of productivity and focus every time you switch tasks.
- Reorienting toward your priorities is work that needs to be done continually. If your to-do list is growing out of control, use a "bubble sort" to make sure the most important tasks bubble to the top and get done first. Be careful about falling into an "everything is an emergency" cycle, and recognize the difference between urgent and important, addressing things in the following order:
    - Important and urgent
    - Important and not urgent
    - Unimportant and urgent
    - Unimportant and not urgent

Chapter 3: Take Control of Your Output

> *"Success isn't always about greatness. It's about consistency. Consistent hard work leads to success. Greatness will come."—Dwayne Johnson*

Imagine that today, the day you're living right now, is a day you will have to repeat forever until the day you die. Whatever you do today, you will have to keep doing. Where will you be in ten years' time? Twenty?

When we're engaged in personal development projects and trying to improve ourselves, it's easy to imagine that someday in the future we'll finally have figured it out. In the future, the things we find difficult right now will all magically be easier, and the laziness and fear we feel today will simply not be an issue tomorrow.

But switch this around and imagine it's the other way: that all you will ever do is what you can manage to do right now, today. This is closer to how things really are. It's what we do every day, consistently, that creates our future. Actions we're planning to do someday, or conditions we're hoping will come about in the future—none of these things are actually going to determine the course of our lives. The only thing that's real is what we do today. Tomorrow, we can do it again, and keep building on that.

This is why it's always, always better to have a very modest but recurring habit instead of a grand overnight makeover project that sounds nice but never actually gets off the ground. It's better to do a small thing a million times over than to try to do a single massive task just once. The small things, the daily actions, are what we can control. We can create a big, impressive life out of small, unimpressive units—and those units are just ordinary days, days like this one.

70:20:10 Technique

For anyone who has ever attempted the grueling task of writing a full-size novel from scratch, they'll know that a very frequent suggestion is to "take care of the quantity, and the quality will take care of itself." In other words, commit to doing your daily habit of, say, one thousand words, and do it no matter what. If you get too hung up on the quality of those words, to the extent that you barely write anything, then you won't get anywhere. This advice sometimes takes the form of "be willing to write badly."

Let's talk about Jonathan Mann, a thirty-eight-year-old songwriter and podcaster based in Hartford, Connecticut, who is known for his "Song a Day" project. He has been writing and recording a song every day since January 1,

2009, and he is probably the best example of putting this principle of "quantity first" into practice.

Inspired by various events and daily occurrences, Mann has now amassed over **4,300 songs**, receiving recognition from the *Guinness Book of World Records* for the most consecutive days spent songwriting. The habit started when he took up an online challenge during a period of unemployment, and it persisted even during challenging moments like being at his grandmother's bedside or experiencing severe food poisoning. Some of Mann's songs have gained mainstream attention, such as "The Baby Yoda Song," which went viral on TikTok.

Mann uses what's now known as the 70:20:10 technique. In other words, quantity breeds quality. Despite acknowledging that not all his songs are hits, with this approach, Mann emphasizes the importance of daily creative practice, no matter what. It's not the quality of the output that is primary, but its quantity, and most especially its consistency. He also cites famous choreographer Martha Graham's advice to "keep the creative channel open"—the idea is that as long as you keep turning up and are receptive, eventually the creative muses will bless you and you will be ready and able to receive that flash of insight.

The 70:20:10 technique, as articulated by Jonathan Mann, is a creative principle applied to endeavors such as songwriting, but can also be applied to any activity that is generative, such as writing, painting, dance, design, and more. It suggests that out of the creative output:

- **Seventy percent will be mediocre:** The majority of the work produced will fall into the category of average or ordinary. These creations may not stand out significantly but contribute to the overall body of work.
- **Twenty percent will suck:** A portion of the output, around one-fifth, will not meet the desired standard. These are creations that may be considered subpar or less impressive.
- **Ten percent will be amazing:** A smaller yet crucial fraction of the work—around one-tenth—will be exceptional or outstanding. These are the pieces that possess unique qualities, creativity, and excellence.

Looking at this ratio, you may be tempted to think that you need to simply endure the average and less-than-average output in order to win the prize of that special and excellent ten percent. This is not quite right; instead, all of your output is valuable and necessary because it is all contributing, in one way or another, to that ten percent. In other words, you cannot skip through the awkward or disappointing parts, because those parts are precisely what allow you to learn and improve. So, this technique is about consistency and habit, but it's also about mindset and managing expectations.

Jonathan Mann emphasizes the importance of not expecting every creation to be a masterpiece, and not being discouraged or resentful when it (inevitably) isn't. The key insight is that through consistent and prolific output, creators increase the likelihood of generating exceptional pieces. The rule is not about choosing between quantity and quality; instead, it emphasizes that quantity, in terms of producing a large volume of work, is instrumental in breeding and enhancing quality.

Applying the 70:20:10 technique to any habit involves embracing a prolific and iterative creative process. In the same way that the four quarters method and the twelve-week year method grant us more opportunities for reflection, adjustment, and growth, the 70:20:10 approach makes sure we're making the most use of our time. Consider the following example.

There are two equally talented songwriters with similar lives and lifestyles. They both have the dream of writing that break-out hit and creating a portfolio of work they're proud of.

Songwriter A is a self-proclaimed perfectionist but lacks tolerance for failure. He hates receiving critical feedback and gets embarrassed by substandard work. So, his solution is to just not produce anything substandard and to aim straight for the masterpiece. He spends a year writing and rewriting the same song, refining it, investing everything into it. The result is:

- A song that is a little better than average.
- One year of time and effort gone.

Songwriter B is passionate but not too afraid to make a fool of himself. He throws himself into projects and starts things up even when he doesn't feel one hundred percent ready or guaranteed of a good outcome. He decides that he can't avoid the awkward learning curve, so he might as well embrace it. He spends a week writing one song and gives himself a deadline, then performs that song whether he's happy with it or not. The next week he does the same.

Just like Songwriter A, most of his efforts are average-ish. Some of his songs are awful and flop badly. But then, about three months in, he writes something that really sparkles. He performs this and it's well received. He keeps going with a song a week, so that by the end of a year, he amasses:

- *Two* genuinely amazing songs.
- Dozens of fairly good/average songs.
- A few embarrassments (which are quickly forgotten because, again, he wrote those two amazing ones).

- One year time and effort gone.

The time and effort spent in both cases is the same. The results are completely different, however. Songwriter A and Songwriter B do not have to have completely different personalities or work schedules. They can put in exactly the same number of hours. The only difference is how they invest that time. The difference is that one has a more frequent "learning cycle," which is a little like throwing the dice again and again—i.e., more chances to win!

There is an obvious irony here. The more someone clings to perfection, the less likely they are to create it. The trick to the 70:20:10 approach is not to become resilient to failure and disappointment, but to realize that it's not something that requires resilience in the first place. "Failing" is not a humiliation or a disaster on the path to learning—it **is** learning. The person who comfortably and easily embraces this learning curve will be the best prepared to keep going, keep producing, keep trying things. Again, we see how often a time management hack is really a mindset hack.

That said, you will not become a master by churning out low-quality, low-effort work again and again. What you do *after* each attempt matters, too. Here's how you can implement this rule in your life.

Step 1: Commit to consistent execution

That is, take care of the quantity. For example, your goal is to be a software engineer. Dedicate a time every day to coding. If you're a budding author, then write. Every single day. If you're an artist trying to produce your magnum opus, then make sure that every day you are doodling, sketching, practicing, working on new pieces.

Consistency is crucial not just for building your skills, but also for developing a diverse portfolio. This collection of work will motivate you when you feel low on inspiration, and can create a sense of purpose and pride. Be humble and expect that you will create boring, unoriginal, or just plain bad work now and again. You're in good company, though—all the masters have done the same. "The master has failed more times than the beginner has tried."

Step 2: Evaluate your output

While it's true that "the quality will take care of itself," you do need to spend some time and effort processing your creations and deliberately learning from them. Periodically assess your body of work. Identify pieces that may not meet the desired standard or fall below your expectations. What's wrong with them? How can you do better? What can you learn from them? How can you take that learning and feed it right back into your next attempt?

This requires another mindset shift. Don't be a useless self-critic who judges their own work simply on whether it's "good" or "not good." Instead, be your own wise mentor and teacher and carefully identify areas of improvement, new avenues for investigation, and signs of evolution. Your goal is not to be impressive or produce something complete and perfect. Your goal is to get fully immersed in the process of creation and become a master of the how, not the what.

Step 3: Identify exceptional pieces

If you follow this approach long enough, sooner or later you will produce something exceptional. Of course, there's no point in doing so unless you're able to recognize when it's happened and respond appropriately. It may be a little more than ten percent or a lot less—what matters is that you are regularly combing through your output and finding that piece that most closely encapsulates the essence, the real mastery, the transcendence of your craft. Analyze what exactly makes these pieces exceptional. Is it a specific style, technique, or subject matter? What did you do differently with this piece, and how can you do more of that?

The wonderful thing about the 70:20:10 approach is that the longer you practice it, the more exceptional pieces you are likely to produce. You create a learning machine that is tuned toward producing these exceptional works. That won't happen, however, unless you have enough work to appraise in the first place, and unless you're actively reflecting and processing what you produce.

A Note on Perfectionism

Sometimes, people will say "I'm such a perfectionist" with more than a hint of pride in their voice. Here's the truth, though: The perfectionist mindset is fragile and unproductive. Perfectionism is not the same as having high standards or being ambitious or meticulous. It's actually all about self-judgment, inflexibility, and fear. The all-or-nothing approach almost always leads to nothing, not all.

If you're a procrastinator or are deathly afraid of failure, then don't be tempted to mask this behind "perfectionism." Instead, commit to actively pursuing imperfection and consciously choose to act despite being ready, and without any assurance that what you do will be great the first time around. Think of it as exposure therapy but for embarrassment—the more you can tolerate being in the less-than-perfect space, the easier it will become, and the more capable you will be of just getting on with the work rather than impotently planning for the work.

For example, imagine that someone has always wanted to make use of their naturally beautiful voice, but never got around to taking lessons and performing in front of others because while their voice is good, it isn't the very best. This person holds a completely unreasonable expectation: that *if they are meant to do something, then it will be easy*. That talent means not having to work hard at something. The natural conclusion, then, is that when this person starts to work on their singing more seriously, they will interpret initial mistakes and imperfections as proof that something is wrong. So, they stop. What has stopped them is not their lack of talent, however, but rather their lack of tolerance for that learning curve that all of us face when embarking on something new. This is the tolerance for failure, embarrassment, and awkwardness.

The really unfortunate thing happens only decades later, when this person meets another singer. This singer began their singing career as someone with less talent, however, because they were willing to tolerate the imperfection of being a learner—they . . . actually learned. Twenty years on, they have a successful and impressive singing career to point to. The first person was and is more naturally talented—but what did it amount to?

This is obviously a very simplified example, but it happens every day in the real world: A person with less talent and ability achieves greater success than a person with more. The successful person's expectation is the reverse of the unsuccessful person's: *"If it's meant to be, it's up to me."*

Picture it this way: We are all signed up for a degree of failure. Even the talented and intelligent must and do fail, usually more than once. The question is, do you want to fail now and get it over and done with, or do you want to do everything you can to avoid it and never fail . . . but only because you never really tried?

It may be a cheesy quote, but "finished is better than perfect." And that's because perfect is not real—it's just an illusion. How many people have gone to their grave with their big idea still inside them, unfulfilled? A dream that is imperfectly brought to life is still real no matter how flawed it is, whereas a fantasy that you get around to someday is worth absolutely nothing.

Manage Your Energy

Ten or twenty years ago, productivity gurus were all about time management. While knowing how to best use your time is a valuable skill, the productivity gurus took a long time to acknowledge something that most of us understood from the beginning: Energy matters, too.

Humans are not machines or simple mathematical algorithms. They're living, breathing organisms with limited and fluctuating energy levels. Today, industrial psychologists and workplace well-being coaches are more likely to frame the matter in terms of stamina, resilience, renewal, and purpose. After all, if a person is depleted, unmotivated, or just plain tired, no time management hack is going to make them more productive.

Big corporations are now realizing that the way to get the most out of their employees is not to work them harder until they burn out, but rather to offer plenty of opportunities for rest, renewal, and reflection. You might be able to force yourself to do more than you physically and emotionally can for a period, but it's a question of diminishing returns. Usually, a runner can go a longer distance if they take a comfortable and sustainable pace, versus if they had spent themselves entirely trying to do it all in a mad sprint.

What does energy management really mean? It means:

- Recognizing that there is nothing intelligent or admirable about pushing yourself to the breaking point.
- Recognizing that a human being is not just their capacity to work; rather, they

are also emotional, social, physical, and spiritual beings.
- Recognizing that there are many ways to be "tired." In other words, pointless, unrewarding, or overly challenging tasks can exhaust you just the same as prolonged tasks, or even more so.
- Similarly, recognizing that there are different types of energy, and they are managed differently.
- Recognizing that we restore and replenish our energy not just so we can quickly deplete ourselves again, but rather because doing so is an *investment* in ourselves and in our work. We don't need to see ourselves as resources to be exploited.
- Recognizing that time is linear, but your experience within that time is extremely malleable. An hour is always an hour, but it has very different values depending on what you do with it.

More practically speaking, energy management is a way of moderating and regulating your activities so that they match and work with your capacity.

Understand and Accommodate Your Own Unique Energy Patterns

Sometimes, timing is everything. As an experiment, track your own energy levels over the course of each day for one whole week. When are you most energetic, productive, and alert? When are you most yearning to rest and reflect? Being aware of your energy levels means acknowledging that it's seldom an on/off scenario, but rather a flow and rhythm. You may naturally be more productive in spring and summer than in winter, you may be more able to do deep work late at night than early in the morning, and you may have unexpected periods now and then of high or low productivity. Just notice how your energy levels tend to rise and fall, but do so without judgment and a mind to "fix" anything.

Gathering this kind of data will allow you to make more informed and conscious choices about when to take a break, when to push yourself, and when to shuffle tasks around. Try to let go of moralistic narratives that paint relentless work as the ideal goal, and instead be curious about how your lifestyle can be tailored to fit your output more comfortably. A dip in energy is not a failure, and a peak in energy is not necessarily your true and most authentic self!

Set Daily Minimums and Maximums for Yourself

Instead of assigning yourself some inflexible demands and goals, identify your maximum energy expenditure limit and establish boundaries to prevent burnout. Just because you are capable of pushing a little further in the short term doesn't necessarily mean you should, or that this is the most optimal way forward. Seek a moderate, manageable pace and ask yourself whether the schedule you've set for yourself for the day could be comfortably repeated for many days and weeks. If not, this is a sign that you're doing too much and that your output is not sustainable. On the other hand, daily minimums help you outline the lower bound of effort to make sure that you're never lowing too much momentum or letting laziness get the better of you.

As an example, you might set an upper bound of never working out for more than forty-five minutes a day, but never doing less than a brisk fifteen-minute walk. This range is realistic and will give you ample wiggle room. On the days you feel especially energetic, you can do the full forty-five minutes, and on days you're feeling tired or unwell, you can still know that you've done a little toward your fitness goals. Of course, it's up to you to decide what is realistic—your upper bound might be someone's bare minimum, and vice versa!

Honor Your Body's Limitations

All human beings cycle through peaks and troughs of energy. Though there is some individual variation, for the most part people have a set pattern for the twenty-four-hour day, and a further, smaller cycle within those twenty-four hours, namely cycles of high and low energy lasting 90 to 120 minutes. If you've spent time identifying your own peaks and troughs, you are then empowered to schedule your most challenging and demanding tasks for your strongest times and leave the lower-effort stuff for periods when you're less alert.

An important part of energy management is body awareness: Pay attention to signs of fatigue, and take a break to recharge before resuming work. In a similar vein, make sure you're doing what you can to ensure a full, restful night's sleep and that you have a consistent sleep/rest schedule, i.e., you wake up and go to sleep at roughly the same time every day.

Pay Attention to ALL Your Energy Sources

You are a complex being that draws its energy and motivation from many sources of vitality:

Physical

Emotional

Mental

Social

Spiritual

Many people who experience burnout do so not because they are mentally depleted or find the work too difficult. Rather, they have run out of emotional and even spiritual resources, and maybe they find their work lacks meaning or social connection. All the workshops and "recovery rooms" the workplace offers them will do nothing to restore them, because these things do not address the nature of their exhaustion.

If you're struggling with energy, motivation, and vitality, ask yourself which of the above energy sources are running low. Are you in poor physical health? Do you need more or less mental challenge in your tasks? Are you feeling sufficiently fulfilled on a deeper, soul level?

One of the most exhausting things in the world is to try to work when you are disillusioned, scared, resentful, bored, or feeling invisible or taken advantage of. If this is you, your energy management will mean addressing these issues first. On the other hand, you could be doing work that is supremely well-aligned to your higher purpose and still not be able to muster energy to work if you are not sleeping, not eating properly, or seriously unfit.

One great idea is to regularly set aside time for yourself to pause and reflect on how you're feeling and how much energy you have. Identify areas of depletion or tiredness, and see what you can do to replenish yourself. Even a quick daily "body and mind scan" in the morning can help you adjust and finetune your schedule as necessary. If rest is necessary, then embrace it fully, without guilt and second-guessing.

Understanding the DRY Principle

The DRY principle, or "Don't Repeat Yourself," is a cornerstone concept in the realm of software development. It advocates for minimizing redundancy in code, emphasizing the creation of reusable components to enhance efficiency and maintainability. By avoiding unnecessary repetition, developers can streamline their codebase, making it more concise and easier to manage.

Beyond the realm of programming, the DRY principle's philosophy can be used in all areas of daily life. Its essence lies in the pursuit of streamlining and efficiency. The idea is to eliminate needless repetition and create a single, authoritative representation of tasks or projects within a system. This approach promotes consistency, organization, and productivity. It also drastically reduces stress and overwhelm.

The genesis of the DRY principle can be traced back to *The Pragmatic Programmer*, a seminal book in software development. It explains, "Every piece of knowledge must have a single, unambiguous, authoritative representation within a system." While this terminology is specific to coding, the underlying concept has some pretty interesting implications. One can substitute "knowledge" with "task" or "project" to understand that each element should have a singular and unambiguous representation—and no more than that.

Good examples of people needlessly "repeating" themselves when it comes to tasks include:

- Writing essentially the same email over and over again to send to different clients or colleagues.
- Running through exactly the same process every month to pay a recurring bill or subscription fee.
- Being the only one who knows how to do something . . . so you're repeatedly the one who does it.

Admittedly, the DRY principle is primarily to do with software code and the written instructions of tasks, rather than the tasks themselves, but looking for redundancies in your own activities will alert you to places where you're spending effort to do a task that, practically speaking, you've already done.

First, Track Your Time

You can only identify redundancies if you have a clear idea of where your time is currently going. Start by keeping a daily journal for at least a week, but you can extend this to a month for a more comprehensive understanding of your routine tasks.

Be specific in the data you gather—this includes identifying both frequent and less frequent occurrences, as well as unplanned or unscheduled tasks such as responding to client emails. Additionally, track monthly and annual tasks like quarterly reports, audits, invoicing, and tech maintenance. By doing so, you gain a bird's-eye view of your tasks, paving the way for the next steps in the DRY process.

Categorize Your Tasks

Once you have a comprehensive view of your tasks, categorize them using your preferred task-tracking tools, such as tags, labels, spreadsheets, or even pen and paper. Identify pain points (you know, the things you procrastinate doing!), bottlenecks, time-consuming tasks, and tasks that involve repetitive work. Your focus should be on identifying repetitive tasks and establishing the ratio between the task's absolute, singular complexity and the time you spend readdressing it.

Create Templates

After categorizing your tasks, focus on areas where repetition occurs. Some repetition is unavoidable, or even desirable. But you won't know until you start tracking with an open mind.

One effective way to eliminate repetitive tasks is by creating templates. These can be blank documents for emails, internal communications, external documents (contracts, proposals, invoices), and presentations. Templates save time by eliminating the need to recreate similar documents daily. Even templates should be thought of as dynamic, however, so make sure you're updating them as needed, or else you are only ensuring that you keep making the same mistake over and over.

Automate Routine Tasks

You don't want to repeat tasks; instead, find ways for tasks to repeat themselves—i.e., automation. If you find yourself doing the same task every single week, is there a way to do it only once and forget about it? You can set up recurring alarms and notifications instead of having to remember anew each time; you can set up direct debits rather than trying to pay bills every month; you can also set up tasks like proposals, invoicing, customer service, and data backup to run on an automated timer.

If a task genuinely does need to be repeated every day and can't be delegated or automated, then try to ease the cognitive load it demands by tacking it onto another habit that runs easily on its own. A classic example is to take important medication whenever you brush your teeth. The habit of teeth brushing is likely well cemented in your mind, so all you have to do is link this to a new behavior. This way you are not expending any extra effort or energy on the additional task.

Teach Yourself to Fish . . . or Even Better, Teach Someone Else

Sometimes, you can save yourself time and effort by asking a seasoned professional to do a specialized job for you. But sometimes it goes the other way around—you save time and effort by learning to do something yourself. For a basic example, you may give yourself the recurring chore of having to rent an expensive piece of equipment, but you immediately make things simpler if you own that piece of equipment yourself.

In a similar way, it may be worth your while to train someone else to do a job that you are wasting too much time doing yourself. Here, consider using the "30x rule" to optimize your daily activities. The rule suggests allocating thirty times the duration of a task for training others to perform that task. It's certainly an investment, but if you are already doing the job more than thirty times yourself, it may be worth it to devote that time to training someone to do it in the long run.

Delegation is great, but it's even more powerful when the tasks you're delegating are ones that repeat themselves. Make the effort to successfully hand over a task to someone else, and it will be the last time you do it. The 30x rule is a strategic approach and is about taking the energy you would use to "repeat yourself" and turning it into an investment in the future.

Summary:

- We are not in control of how naturally talented we are and cannot always guarantee that our work will be brilliant or amazing. What we can do is commit to consistency in our actions. By following the 70:20:10 technique, we understand that quantity breeds quality, and that if we just keep producing, eventually the brilliant and amazing will come: approximately seventy percent of what we produce will be mediocre, twenty percent will be poor, but ten percent will be something special. Consistency means continually creating and continually choosing to learn from what we do, whether it works out well or not.
- Perfectionism is extremely toxic and will undermine your efforts, especially if it lowers your tolerance for failure or the awkwardness that is part of every learning journey. Successful people do not fail less!
- How you manage your time and attention is extremely important, but energy matters too. Pay attention to your own unique energy

patterns and rhythms, and work with rather than against your body. Set limits for yourself to preserve your energy rather than deplete and exploit yourself as a resource. Recognize, too, that there are different types of energy and consequently different ways to be fatigued; understanding this means you can address tiredness and burnout correctly. Set daily minimums and maximums and honor them no matter what.

- Finally, don't repeat yourself (DRY). Pay attention to any repetitive tasks and use automation, delegation, or templates to make sure you're not doing the same task over and over.

Chapter 4: Take Control of Your Environment

"It is better for you to take responsibility for your life as it is, instead of blaming others, or circumstances, for your predicament. As your eyes open, you'll see that your state of health, happiness, and every circumstance of your life has been, in large part, arranged by you—consciously or unconsciously." —Dan Millman

In this chapter, we're going to be taking a good look at excuses—i.e., all the strange names we give to our own decision not to take the action we know we should.

The list of reasons people can't be more disciplined and productive is literally infinite:

- I have a busy and demanding job, and I just don't have enough time for [x].
- I'm raising a family and I'm too exhausted for [x].
- I'd love to [x], but I don't have enough money.

- Other people are holding me back.
- The place I live in is holding me back.
- My past is holding me back.
- It's too cold today.
- It's Sunday.
- I'm tired.
- Meh.

All of the above are ways of blaming, essentially, the environment for *our choices* or lack thereof. It is entirely true that we are influenced by the environment we find ourselves in. But we always seem to forget that we can also influence our environment!

We can move, we can make new friends, we can change jobs, we can fix our lifestyles . . . we can put on a sweater. We never have complete control over absolutely everything—but we never have so little to justify taking no action.

One big excuse that may come up for you is one that is partly a good reason and partly a bad excuse: "I can't do [x] because I don't know where to start. I'm uncertain/overwhelmed/stressed." Luckily, there's a lot we can do to make our world feel clearer and easier to navigate.

Combat Uncertainty with Clarity

Many people talk about procrastination as though it is a problem in its own right. However, procrastination is not a problem; it's a *symptom* of a problem, and until you have a clear understanding of what that problem is, you will continue to procrastinate. We may embark on a task and find ourselves wavering, afraid, overwhelmed, or confused. Then we hesitate and fail to take action. What happens next is how we interpret this hesitation—we may conclude that we are lazy or undisciplined. But is that really the problem?

Procrastination is a symptom that accompanies many quite different problems, but one common one is a lack of certainty. This kind of procrastination can be better understood as "uncertainty paralysis," a phenomenon that occurs when individuals are unclear about their tasks, their goals, their purpose, and so on. Most of us tend to just assume that if there is a task in front of us, all the big *why* and *what* questions have already been answered, and we simply need to dive in and get started.

Sometimes, however, our repeated inability to get started with something may be telling us something important—not about our own laziness or lack of discipline, but about how poorly we have defined the task at hand.

We may then make all sorts of complicated excuses and waste time engaging with those excuses, when the real problem is that we lack clarity and certainty. For example, we blame our job or the company that we work for when the real trouble is that we don't have enough clarity about how to do that job, or we blame others for taking up all our time or getting in our way, when the real problem is that we have not clearly understood our own time limits and failed to schedule realistically. What I'm saying is that a lack of uncertainty can end up being masked in all sorts of ways and can hide behind plenty of convincing excuses.

Of course, nothing in life is one hundred percent certain, and all of us have to act at some point even though we're not working with all the information we need and aren't guaranteed any particular outcome. What's more, people naturally vary in their tolerance for uncertainty, between one another and even within themselves, depending on the task.

If you've got an ongoing issue with procrastination, however, it might be worth asking if you can do more to work directly with uncertainty and *not* with your discipline, motivation, or personal sense of purpose.

Having a low uncertainty tolerance will mean you experience more anxiety, but it also means you may perceive certain risks and dangers as more significant than they are, think that the stakes are higher than they are, or avoid taking action in an effort to avoid perceived danger.

On the other hand, having a high uncertainty tolerance means you are more resilient and cope better. It means you are able to appraise threat and risk more clearly and accurately and take action when it's right to do so.

If procrastination is a problem for you, it may either be that you have too low a tolerance for uncertainty, but it could also be that you are currently living and working within an environment that is way more chaotic and confusing than it needs to be—i.e., *the task itself is not the problem, but your lack of clarity about the task is the problem.* If you try to force yourself to take action while you lack clarity, all you do is create resentment and fatigue.

Ali Abdaal is a productivity expert and author of *Feel-Good Productivity: How to Do More of What Matters to You*. Abdaal's big idea is that the single best way to make yourself more productive is to make yourself feel good—i.e., negative emotions may motivate you in the short term, but it's positive emotions that keep you sustainably engaged and creative. From his point of view, discipline is not about becoming your own slave driver, but about learning to find sources of energy that can be converted into meaningful work, at the same time as removing blocks and obstacles. What you cannot do, he explains, is force yourself through those obstacles, all the while feeling negative.

In his program he recommends building up an inner reserve of good feelings by playing (i.e., incorporating fun and stress relief into daily life), building your confidence and sense of empowerment, and making sure that we're surrounding ourselves with people who inspire and motivate us.

When it comes to procrastination, the root cause can certainly be inertia and laziness, but it may more likely be a lack of courage or a lack of clarity. You need to be certain of WHY you're doing a task, WHAT the task actually is, and WHEN you are supposed to be doing it. The next time you find yourself dragging your feet on a project, double-check to see if any of these three areas are lacking clarity. You may be surprised!

Let's take a closer look.

WHY Are You Doing the Task?

You want to consider the high-level reasons and purpose behind this activity, but think about the mid- and lower-level answers to this question as well. If motivation and passion are lacking, check to see that you're not working toward somebody else's goals, or going ahead with something without truly understanding how it connects to your broader intentions and values.

One potential problem is that you have an overarching goal but have gradually lost sight of it over time and need to stop, reappraise, and remind yourself of the bigger picture. A bigger potential problem is that you never considered those overarching goals in the first place. Once the initial excitement of a new goal wore off, you were left with little enthusiasm for it because it did not connect in any meaningful way to a larger purpose.

The "five whys" technique is one way to get to the bottom of resistant, avoidant, or unmotivated behavior such as procrastination. You simply keep asking yourself "Why?" to drill down to the deeper reasons. For example, you keep putting off studying for your exam. You ask:

Why do you not want to study?

Because I'm too tired!

Why are you too tired?

I guess because I didn't sleep well last night.

Why didn't you sleep well?

Because I was in bed and scrolling through social media on my phone.

Why were you doing that?

Because I'm stressed out and need the distraction. It helps me relax.

Why are you so stressed out and unrelaxed?

Because I'm not studying!

Okay, so that's an overly simple example, but you get the idea. In this case, you can see that the five whys often illuminate a vicious cycle element to your problem. In either case, it will help you understand what is standing in your way, and therefore what you need to do to remove that roadblock. In this example, it might be worth investigating healthier ways to cope with stress (crucially, it's not a discipline problem, but an anxiety problem). In Abdaal's model, this looks like deliberately cultivating positive feelings like relaxation and human connection—and in a healthy form that doesn't cause you to lose out on sleep!

WHAT Exactly Are You Doing?

Sometimes we can get majorly fired up about a new project or task, only for that motivation to come grinding to a halt the moment we need to take practical first steps. This is usually because we do not have a clear enough understanding of the concrete, real-world actions we need to take. The reason and purpose are there, but it's not translating into the real world properly.

Here, your twelve-week year planning can come in handy again as you break down tasks into smaller and more manageable chunks. Also consider spending a little time thinking about the practical obstacles you're likely to face, and how you might get around them.

SMART goals are always useful, but consider setting NICE goals, too.

The four key principles of NICE goals are:

Near-Term Goals:

Focus on intermediate steps rather than being overwhelmed by distant objectives.

Example: Instead of a long-term weight-loss goal, set a daily goal of exercising for thirty minutes.

Input-Based Goals:

Emphasize the process over the final outcome, making progress more manageable.

Example: Rather than fixating on losing weight in six months, set an input goal like going for a ten-minute walk every day.

Controllable Goals:

Concentrate on goals within one's control, considering the busy nature of life.

Example: If writing a book, opt for controllable goals, such as a specific word count, or a time-related goal, such as writing for twenty minutes.

Energizing Goals:

Integrate elements of play and work to make tasks enjoyable and boost confidence.

Example: Enhance the experience by listening to music while working, or using colorful stationery you love.

So, a career-related SMART goal may be: "Get a promotion to a senior management position within two years," whereas a NICE goal would be: "Dedicate an hour each week to improving a key skill or networking."

Even as you read the two goals above, you might already get a feel for which feels more achievable—and this all comes down to clarity.

WHEN Will You Do All This?

Once you have identified the tasks required, you need to schedule them and assign them a place in your overall workflow. It sometimes happens that we are not being lazy or unproductive, but rather just impatient! We have failed to have realistic expectations about how long something will take and how much effort it will require.

Adopt an Incremental Approach:

Level 1: Schedule specific tasks like appointments.

Level 2: Use day theming and the 52:17 method to organize your day around your tasks.

Level 3: Regularly reappraise your progress and adjust as you go.

Overcoming uncertainty involves a strategic blend of understanding the purpose ("why"), setting effective goals ("what"), and scheduling tasks ("when"). Addressing these three areas drastically reduces feelings of uncertainty and makes it far less likely that we will procrastinate.

That said, remember that a certain degree of uncertainty is unavoidable. Once you have done your very best to find clarity, purpose, and focus, realize that any remaining uncertainty will have to be tolerated. Remind yourself that sometimes we think we need to delay acting until we feel courageous and motivated enough, but the opposite is true: It's only by taking action that we build our courage and our motivation.

Write a To-Don't List

Renowned trust and technology expert Rachel Botsman advocates for a "to-don't list," stemming from recognizing the never-ending nature of traditional to-do lists. Despite their ubiquity and popularity, to-do lists can become overwhelming and lead to burnout as tasks accumulate continuously. You can begin to feel resentful of this little piece of paper making demands on you that never really seem to stop.

Botsman emphasizes the finite nature of time, prompting people to consider what they can *subtract* from their commitments rather than solely focusing on additions. The effect is to create, you guessed it, more clarity. More focus. More calm.

The continuous influx of tasks, particularly in professional settings, can create a sense of being trapped in an ever-expanding workload, like a rat on a wheel. If psychologically you know that achieving your tasks is only ever rewarded with more tasks, things can quickly start to feel pointless.

Botsman's idea is simple: Create a "to-don't list," which is nothing more than **a list of tasks or habits that you never, ever do**. The goal is to eliminate all those distracting, low-value tasks from your life, put up firm boundaries, and delegate if necessary. This is great for anyone struggling with self-discipline because there's no thinking and no effort required: Is a task on your to-don't list? Then don't do it, end of story. You don't need to coax yourself or weigh up pros and cons or get into shame spirals about what you should and shouldn't be doing. You decide for yourself—once—what doesn't matter, and then you enjoy the peace of mind that comes with not having to mentally process that again.

The mindset shift is subtle but powerful: Understanding that time and energy are limited, you proactively switch your focus to what matters, rather than constantly feeling that you are being chased by obligations you'd rather just avoid.

What should go on your to-don't list? Anything that you know in your gut is something you shouldn't be wasting time on but tend to waste time on anyway. Things like:

- Distractions, addictions, amusements, diversions
- Tasks that aren't really adding anything to your life
- Tasks you're doing for other people, but you shouldn't
- Bad habits that physically, emotionally, or mentally drain you
- Pointless busy work that doesn't need to be done in the first place

Central to Botsman's to-don't list is the consideration of energy. Rather than focusing on specific categories, she reflects on how she spends her time, with whom, and what she wants to prioritize—and, equally importantly, what to avoid. This mindful energy allocation enables her to make intentional choices about where to invest her efforts, preventing the temptation to continually add tasks to an already burdened schedule. This approach helps her stay focused on tasks that hold the greatest significance in her work and life.

Examples from her to-don't list include not working with misaligned clients, not undervaluing easy tasks, avoiding meetings during certain hours, refraining from social media after 7 p.m., resisting others' agendas, and even avoiding specific individuals. This monthly reflection helps Botsman prioritize her energy and stay focused on meaningful work, fostering mindfulness about where she directs her efforts.

Tasks put on this list are either deleted, delegated, outsourced, or outright rejected when they attempt to make their way onto your to-do list. It's important that you don't waste time apologizing, making excuses, or justifying anything—you don't want to waste *any* time engaging with the task.

The primary goal of a well-crafted to-don't list is to streamline your efforts and concentration, ensuring that you engage only in tasks that contribute the highest value. By actively avoiding or eliminating less important or distracting activities, you create room for meaningful and impactful work. The aim is to be more realistic in your focus, striving to dedicate your time to the most crucial tasks at least eighty percent of the time.

Here's how to use Botsman's method yourself:

Step 1: Take time to make the list

Allocate a dedicated thirty to sixty minutes to create your to-don't list. Recognize that investing time in this initial phase will lead to significant time savings in your everyday life. Consider it a proactive measure to streamline your tasks and enhance productivity.

Step 2: Analyze your tasks from the previous months

Engage in retrospective analysis by reviewing your past tasks, particularly those that recur. Open your calendar, check your to-do lists, or use time-tracking software to identify patterns in your personal and professional responsibilities. This step lays the foundation for understanding your task dynamics.

Step 3: Identify the tasks that should be on your to-don't list

Conduct a thorough evaluation of each recurring task. Assess the impact of each task on your future and question the value it adds. Explore opportunities to delete, delegate, or outsource tasks, freeing up time for more high-value activities. Reflect on your emotional responses during task performance, noting negative feelings, procrastination tendencies, guilt, or anger.

Basically, you want to identify the tasks that are draining on a daily basis and aren't moving you toward what you want to be doing. If you're still unsure what to add to your list, vet your list by asking yourself some simple questions about the task:

- Will my daily life keep rolling along as usual if I don't do this?
- Can I delegate this task to someone else?
- Does doing this task always drag me down?
- Does this task even need to be done?

Step 4: Learn how to say no

Recognize that saying no is often the most challenging part of the process. Develop the skill to decline tasks, having the courage to say no both to yourself and to others. Regularly review and update your to-don't list—at least every quarter—to adapt to changes in your life situation and maintain its relevance.

Take the pressure off and reorient yourself toward your values, your purpose, and the small set of priorities you are choosing to focus on. Sometimes we just need to pause long enough to ask, "Hang on a second, do I really care about this? Is this really important in the grand scheme?" A to-don't list is simply a more formalized way of asking yourself these questions.

Bear in mind Steve Jobs's advice: "People think focus means saying yes to the thing you've got to focus on. But that's not what it means at all. It means saying no to the hundred other good ideas that there are. Innovation is saying no to one thousand things."

The following is an example list:

- Don't spend more than an hour on social media a day
- Don't gossip
- Don't eat heavily processed foods
- Don't allow other people to rush you
- Don't check your email first thing in the morning
- Don't "doomscroll"
- Don't answer unrecognized phone numbers
- Don't spend time with energy-draining individuals
- Don't think about work during your "me time"
- Don't go to a meeting that has no clear agenda

As you practice putting together your own list, you may start to notice that it begins to resemble a kind of personal mission statement, or a list of values and principles. That's because it is! A personal code is a time-saving device and a tool to make your life simpler and easier. In the spirit of not repeating yourself, a to-don't list asks you to figure out what you do and don't value *once*, and then to stick to it. Procrastination, resentment, and anxiety about work are all just different ways of wasting your own time, after all.

Build a "Good Habit Machine"

What is a good habit, at the end of the day?

It's a particular kind of behavior—i.e., one that is automatic. When it comes to making good changes to our lives, many of us understandably get caught up in the *effort* and willpower required to do something different, but the truth is we should be focused more on the process rather than the outcome. If we are patient and consistent enough, in other words, certain good behaviors will become automatic, and then the question of "discipline" becomes irrelevant, because we do the optimal thing automatically.

How do you make the optimal behavior automatic? How can you make it so that the best action is always the easiest, most involuntary one?

In this section we'll consider the power of creating an environment that actively elicits and supports the kind of behavior you want to maintain into the future—in other words, the kind of environment that acts like a "good habit machine."

It takes a mindset shift to begin thinking this way, but try to imagine that the environment around you is itself capable of "choosing" and "thinking." If you are aware only of the ways in which you as an isolated individual are making conscious choices, you miss out on all the ways you could be optimizing your environment so that it, too, helps make the right move feel like the easiest and most obvious move.

An ideal environmental "good habit machine" is one that works on conditioning—that is, punishment and reward. In behavioral psychology, this is precisely what learning is: adapting to stimuli in the environment. A behavior that is followed by a reward is more likely to be a behavior that is repeated, while one that is followed by a punishment is less likely to be repeated.

As mature and rational adults, you might know on one level that there is an abstract reward for your behaviors. For example, you know that if you exercise diligently and watch your diet, you will see weight loss and gains in strength. But these rewards are distant and abstract and so tend not to motivate our behavior as strongly.

A great book on habit and behavior change, called *Changing for Good*, underscores the pivotal role of environmental controls and rewards during the action and maintenance stages of behavior change. The book advocates for modifying both **cues** and **consequences** to fortify positive behaviors, and stresses the significance of celebrating progress at each step—acknowledging and celebrating your progress is, of course, a major way to positively reinforce your behavior.

All this talk of behavior modification and reward/punishment may make you think of Pavlov's dogs or a rat in a maze, but we humans are subject to all the same behavioral laws. We may be more complex than dogs or rats, but we still follow all the same principles that they do! Our goals may be more sophisticated and abstract, but in many ways, we pursue them in much the same way as they pursue theirs.

Where humans have an edge, however, is that we can stand outside of this process and actively engineer it for ourselves. We can make sure that we are the ones pulling the levers of reward so that we are, in effect, training ourselves. Rather than this being a limiting and deterministic way of looking at things, it is actually an empowering stance to take—a way of consciously working *with* your animal brain rather than trying to valiantly fight *against* it.

The key to building an environment that actively encourages the best of you is actually awareness. To build more awareness, you need to get into the habit of tracking and monitoring your behavior. It doesn't matter whether you do this through complicated spreadsheets or a simple journal; the key is that you are *watching*. This self-awareness serves as a catalyst for heightened self-control, significantly enhancing the likelihood of successful change.

Frequently checking in with yourself and your goals contributes to your goals not only because it gives you an opportunity to adjust and adapt, but also because it gives you the opportunity to reward yourself. In other words, tracking leads to awareness of progress leads to celebration leads to reward leads to . . . more of the same behavior that led to the progress in the first place.

If you never pause long enough to acknowledge how much you've achieved, you never give your brain the chance to experience this outcome as positive at all. You miss a crucial opportunity to reinforce the right behavior, and you just blast through to the next slog or challenge. If you pause and celebrate, though, you are telling your brain, "Yes! That's good! We like this. Let's do more of it."

This is why small, frequent rewards are so much more powerful than a single reward at the very end—because small rewards offer you more "reps" to reinforce the desired behavior.

External rewards, originating from external sources, and internal rewards, self-generated and personal, both play pivotal roles in the process of behavior change. Tangible rewards, encompassing items or activities, and intangible rewards, such as positive self-talk or personal affirmations, contribute to a well-rounded approach. The narrative underscores the importance of identifying meaningful progress points and emphasizes the utilization of charts for monitoring progress, applicable to both health and wealth goals.

Here's how you can start to use the principle of reward to create an environment that rewards precisely the kind of behavior you're trying to cultivate.

Step 1: Use the "shaping up" technique by determining short-term goals (e.g., five-pound weight loss) that contribute to your ultimate goal (e.g., fifty-pound weight loss).

Reinforce positive behavior at each "milestone" or completion of a short-term goal. Find a way, if possible, to build this milestone check into your everyday schedule—i.e., the environment itself should continually prompt you to monitor and reward your behavior.

You could do this by programming an alarm or reminder at the same time every day or week to encourage you to pause and measure your progress. Depending on what you're trying to achieve, you can keep visual reminders in your environment that will keep your goal top of mind. In the weight loss example, you could enlist the help of an "accountability buddy" at work (whom you cannot avoid even if you tried!) and commit to a weekly check-in with them. You could put inspiring quotes, collages, or charts on your fridge or in the bathroom so you can see them every day when you have a shower, etc.

You'll need a little creativity here; the idea is simply to make the environment do the heavy lifting for you until your chosen behavior becomes more automatic. If, for example, you want to get into the habit of taking a certain supplement every morning, then place it right next to your toothbrush where you can see it. You spend no additional cognitive effort to brush your teeth every morning, so by linking this new habit up to an old one, your environment is "choosing" for you. You'll know you're on the right track when you have to actively spend effort to *not* do something that your environment is making inevitable.

Step 2: Think about your progress indicators

Tracking your progress is good. *How* you track progress depends on how and what you measure. If you've made SMART goals, you should already be familiar with choosing metrics that are specific, realistic, and so on. If you are trying to lose weight, for instance, you have the option to track pounds lost, but you could also track clothing sizes or inches. On the other hand, your goal may be more appropriately expressed in terms of process—i.e., you monitor how many miles you can walk, how many resumes you sent off, how many calories you ate, or how many hours you spent reading that week.

Don't assume that the first way you think of measuring is necessarily the best one. For example, some people find that weighing themselves every day and agonizing over every single pound is simply too much and counterproductive. Instead, they focus on pound increments but weigh themselves every week or even every month. You may find that you are more disciplined keeping to a reading habit when your goal is "read ten pages" and not "read for thirty minutes" . . . or vice versa. The point is simply that the way you track and measure is itself something that you can optimize. What gets measured gets improved. All the more reason to think very carefully about *exactly* what you're measuring!

Step 3: Chart your progress

A chart is a great way to visualize your progress. Remember that a lack of clarity can create inertia and a sense of procrastination. But if you can clearly *see* the path ahead and your progress on it, then you are far more likely to be inspired to take the next step. Charting is especially helpful when the goal is very large, or when it feels a little more abstract. Weight loss, for example, is often not felt or seen on the body until it's well underway. You might not be able to see the results and may not feel compelled to celebrate them. The habit may not be reinforced, and you could give up.

But if you create an external, visual representation of the weight you've lost, you can see that you have in fact moved closer to your goal and can celebrate that. It's far less likely you'll throw in the towel.

The way you choose to visualize your process is up to you. Options include making graphs where you plot your score on a daily or weekly basis, but here you can also be extremely creative. You could, for example, put a penny in a jar for every multiple of ten dollars that you put in a savings account. It might not feel very satisfying or rewarding to deposit virtual money directly into a savings account, but if you can *see* an indication of that jar steadily filling up with coins, it's far more motivating.

You could also try a kind of reverse chart, wherein what you're tracking is the absence of a behavior. For example, if you're giving up cigarettes or a bad social media habit, create an "X many days since bad behavior" style chart, where you can steadily see the number growing bigger the more you stay on track. The bigger that number, the more motivated you are to maintain your "winning streak."

Step 4: Reflect and reinforce

The final step is where you reward all that good behavior! Think of your reward as a kind of bright-yellow highlighter that moves retrospectively through your life and highlights all those behaviors you want to keep on repeating. These are the things you're choosing to retain from the past and do again . . . and again and again.

When you reward yourself, you are creating a feeling of positivity and accomplishment that is, essentially, addictive. Every time you pair this positive feeling with a desired action, you are teaching yourself to *want* to take that action again—no discipline required! Understanding things this way, you more easily understand the difference between a reward that is healthy and supportive, and one that isn't.

You can certainly reward yourself with a sweet treat, a material item, or the afternoon off, for example, but what matters is not the treat or the item, but the positive feelings you're able to conjure. Many people drastically underestimate how amazing it can feel just to pause and enjoy a little self-praise for a job well done.

Where possible, try to make your rewards stem organically from your progress. For a very obvious example, consider the goal of losing weight. You may achieve impressive weight loss over the course of a month . . . and then decide to reward yourself with a big weekend binge that undoes all your hard work. A better reward would be a sincere compliment from a close friend, a delicious but still healthy dinner out, or buying yourself an item of clothing you wouldn't have had the confidence to wear before.

Internal and External Rewards

It's a great idea to incorporate a combination of *external* rewards (those provided by the environment or other people) and *internal* rewards (those that are self-generated).

Examples of external rewards include financial incentives from an accountability buddy or the aforementioned sincere compliment from someone you trust and respect. Internal rewards can be tangible (e.g., purchasing items with savings) or intangible (e.g., engaging in activities like a relaxing bubble bath or positive self-talk).

Which style of reward is better? They both work. There is nothing intrinsically wrong with external motivation, especially for those tasks that you are honestly not going to muster any real love for. A good rule of thumb is to use external rewards to get you started, and internal ones to maintain you over the long term. For example, you might have had a flash of vanity and wanted to lose weight so you could impress an old fling at a high school reunion (one hundred percent external reward!), but that doesn't mean you can't also tap into a more internally generated desire for better health and well-being long after the reunion is over.

Summary:

- It's easy to make excuses and blame the environment around us for why we can't be more disciplined, but although the world influences us, we can also influence it. If we find that we are lacking clarity, then it's time to make the environment around us clearer by asking
    - Why are you doing the task?
    - What exactly are you doing?
    - When will you do it?

  This will give you focus and direction and stop you from getting hung up on reasons why you can't act.
- To better understand **why** you're doing a task, or why a problem is occurring, use the "five whys" technique. If motivation and passion are lacking, check in on your higher-level purpose.
- To better understand **what** you're doing, set both SMART and NICE goals to bring the dream to reality, especially if you're having trouble with losing momentum.
- To better understand **when** you will do a task, schedule tasks in your calendar and be patient!
- A to-don't list is a list of tasks you never do, and it's a way to manage your environment and take responsibility for your values and

principles, rather than blaming the distractions.
- Build a "good habit machine" so your environment is actively and automatically making your desired behavior more likely. Give yourself frequent opportunities for both internal and external rewards to reinforce behavior. Be mindful of the progress indicators you're using, chart your progress, and regularly reflect on your progress.

Chapter 5: Take Control of Your Emotions and Mindset

"The concept of emotional intelligence suggests that intelligence may understand emotion, and that emotion may facilitate intelligence." —Joseph Ciarrochi, Joseph Forgas, and John Mayer (2006).

Not knowing how to handle negative emotions like fear, shame, and overwhelm can derail your life. They can undermine your deepest held ambitions and cut your potential in half.

But if you re-read the above, you'll notice that it's not that *negative emotions* themselves can sabotage you; rather, it's the *inability to handle them* that causes us so much trouble.

You could be forgiven for thinking that discipline and self-control are all about suppression and learning to squash down and ignore all those messy, uncomfortable feelings. The opposite is true, though. People who are effective, productive, and poised do not have fewer negative emotions than anyone else; they've just learned how to manage them wisely.

Mastering your emotions is not about becoming a cold, invulnerable robot. Rather, it's about learning to understand and use your own feelings consciously and intelligently.

Rapid Planning Method

In Tony Robbins's workbook *Time of Your Life*, he explains his RPM—Rapid Planning Method, like this:

> *"The first step toward taking back your focus and achieving the realization of your vision is to ask yourself three questions in a specific sequence on a consistent basis, the RPM system. Although RPM stands for the Rapid Planning Method, you can also think of it as a Results-Oriented/Purpose-Driven/Massive Action Plan.*
>
> *The sequence is critical, because if you don't know what you want, why you want it, and then create a plan for how to get to it, in that order, your actions will not be sustainable through life's challenges, and*

you'll have little possibility of experiencing what it is you truly desire."

This evolved way of thinking grants you the pleasure of experiencing the goal fulfillment you've always envisioned for yourself. There are three distinct steps that you must take to step into the RPM's management technique."

The Rapid Planning Method is a straightforward time management approach designed to enhance productivity and achieve goals. It emphasizes clear objectives, purposeful actions, and continual progress toward success. According to Robbins, RPM is a thinking system rather than a mere time management tool, aiming to create a fulfilling and constantly evolving life. This technique encourages individuals to explore their full potential.

Let's take a closer look at the acronym:

Results-Oriented (R): What do I really want?

Purpose-Driven (P): Why does it matter to me?

Massive Action Plan (M): How will I achieve it?"

As we've already seen, Robbins's approach is not all that different from the why/what/when approach covered in Chapter 4, and will help you gain more clarity and focus.

Here, there are those pesky negative emotions to think about!

These negative emotions can get in the way of each stage of the process, and if we want to get the best out of our efforts, we will have to proactively recognize that obstacle ... so we can step right over it. If you are too overwhelmed by the process, if you're filled with fear, if your self-esteem is low, the process won't work, just as it won't work if you're a perfectionist, afraid to commit, or just too hard on yourself. The following process, then, is just as much about what you do as what you choose not to do—i.e., the negative emotions you refuse to entertain.

Step 1—Get everything out of your head and onto a piece of paper

Write down everything you need or want to accomplish. To stay true to the "rapid" element, you might like to use the Pomodoro Technique and limit this step to around twenty-five minutes maximum.

The negative emotion that might derail your efforts here is *overwhelm*. True discipline will look like consciously deciding to limit how much you can tackle with your available mental bandwidth. This is what this step is all about—

by slowing down and forcing your thoughts into black and white, you concretize and cut down on the anxiety that comes with endless rumination. If you're feeling like there are a million things whizzing around your head and you're not sure where to start, start here. Make it a game—put everything down on a page, but stop at that twenty-five-minute mark and move on.

Step 2—Chunk things down until they're manageable

Organize tasks into categories and prioritize them, aiming for no more than three to five outcomes. Then, use SMART goals to create smaller, more manageable short- and mid-term goals. Doing this helps you overcome another self-sabotaging negative emotion: *fear*.

If you're feeling totally intimidated by the prospect of a new task or project, that's usually a sign that it's just too big. This is the kind of fear that has us doubting our own abilities and feeling as though we're not up to the task. But this is usually an illusion; we see how big the gap is between where we are and where we want to be, and can't visualize how we will ever cover that distance.

Chunking things down decreases that perceived distance and suddenly makes you feel as though you *do* have what it takes to tackle the task head-on. If you're feeling afraid, intimidated, or in over your head, then this is the step you need to focus on the most—keep chunking down until you're looking at a task that feels doable. Not easy, no, but achievable.

Step 3—"Massively plan with purpose"

Tony Robbins is a big proponent of the power of purpose and tapping into the almost infinite energy supply that your own sense of meaning can provide you. Tasks that are not connected to your purpose in any way are like appliances that are unplugged—they're useless. There's nothing powering them.

You can probably see how this step most elegantly addresses a major category of negative emotions when it comes to discipline and productivity, and that is *a lack of motivation and passion*. We all have to do work we find boring or difficult at times, but if you're consistently finding that you have no energy or impetus for a task, then you may be missing out on this crucial step of the process.

Why are you doing what you're doing? What's the point? What does it all mean? If you don't have an answer to these questions, you may find yourself stalling out of sheer apathy and disinterest. Another possibility is that you are stuck in a loop of dreaming too small. This is why Robbins recommends massive planning—be ambitious, step out of your comfort zone, and set yourself an audacious, exciting goal. You can do this if—and only if—you connect that goal to your purpose.

Step 4—Take action . . . and make that action the foundation of your new identity

Habits and actions shape your identity. What you do consistently every day shapes your future. It shapes who you *are*. The biggest source of self-sabotage here is a *lack of commitment*. Many people have no trouble being disciplined for a week or a month or even six months. They don't maintain their gains, however, because, deep down, they continue to think of the behavior as temporary, and they cling to their old identity—the undisciplined one—as who they "really are." This is a crisis of commitment because they have not truly made the mental leap and dedicated themselves to the goal.

A lack of commitment can more commonly appear as simply laziness. You may be all too ready to flesh out an elaborate fantasy of yourself as some new person with dazzling new habits, but unless you take consistent, meaningful action toward building that identity for yourself, a fantasy is all it will ever be.

If you find that you are uncertain, undecided, or somehow wishy-washy about your new goal, what you are lacking is likely not inspiration or purpose, but commitment. Everything can be perfectly aligned and ready to go, but nothing will happen unless you *commit* to it, and that means taking action, then taking action again, and then continuing to take it day after day.

Step 5—Review

As we've seen, the review stage is an important part of the process because it's where we reflect and reward the behavior we want to keep and amplify in the future. This is what keeps us motivated, helps us learn, and makes us feel capable and confident. There are sadly plenty of negative emotions that can disrupt your efforts at this stage.

If you are battling feelings of low self-worth, if you're filled with *judgment and self-loathing*, or if you can't forgive failures and move on from them, you are seriously limiting your capacity to grow and evolve. Instead of using the reward of positive emotion to keep you moving in the right direction, you use negative emotion to keep you chained to what isn't working, and trapped in states of mind that aren't serving you.

At this stage, Robbins recommends that you ask some pointed, but neutral questions to reflect on your progress. Did you follow the steps you assigned for yourself? Why or why not? Did your purpose motivate you? Did you achieve the desired result? What worked? What didn't work?

Beware, however, that these questions should never lean toward condemnation or judgment. If you've made a mistake or taken a wrong turn, acknowledge it plainly and immediately commit to taking action in the right direction. Dwelling on how awful you are only prolongs the negativity and makes you less likely to gain any useful insight from the experience.

Rewarding the good is necessary, but so is forgiving the bad. It is more important to know how to gracefully move on from a setback or slip-up than it is to avoid setbacks and slip-ups in the first place. Realize that your power lies in your *response* to these things.

Emotional Self-Regulation

As you get better at tracking and monitoring your progress, as your goal-setting ability becomes more sophisticated, and as your skill at cultivating good habits grows stronger, you will find that managing your emotions is as important as managing your time, your energy, or your finances.

Rather than seeing negative emotions as unwelcome intruders, learn to look at them as a natural part of life and valuable messengers. If, for example, you notice yourself feeling resentful, dig a little deeper into the experience and try to understand why. Are you overly tired but still pushing yourself? You may need to take a break. If you notice that you're continually feeling scattered and confused about your work, then this may be a signal to stop and inquire further. Could your organization be better? Are you responding to a lack of clarity in the way the task has been conceptualized?

Too often, self-help material encourages us to do the opposite—i.e., if we're tired, push on, if we're scared, feel the fear and do it anyway. You may find it much easier and more effective, however, to adopt a genuinely compassionate and curious attitude to your own emotions and listen to what information they could be conveying. Sometimes, procrastination is a warning flag that we have strayed from our purpose. Sometimes, a lack of productivity is because we're challenging ourselves too much or too little. Which one is it? The only way to know is to stop and pay attention. This is the irony of emotional self-regulation—the more you actively engage with your emotions, the less you have to deal with them!

Hyperfocus and Scatterfocus

Picture this: Person A gets up early one morning and sits down at their desk, cracks their knuckles, and is soon knee-deep in their work. They're like a machine, super focused on what's in front of them, blasting through challenge after challenge, and totally absorbed in that coveted "flow" state where you feel like you're on fire.

Sounds good, right? This is what many of us imagine when we think of a productive and disciplined person. But now picture someone else, Person B, who gets up three hours after Person A, then goes for a walk on the beach. They then sit for fifteen minutes on a log, examining shells and stones, thinking. They hum a little song, scribble some lines in the sand, then head home. Once at their desk, they pick up pen and paper and start doodling, but soon the crayons come out too, and then they're pacing the room, talking to themselves, even miming out a few ideas as they occur. This is the classic nutty professor archetype we're all familiar with, and most of us have seen enough movies to know that the creative genius is usually doing something completely random and bizarre right before the eureka moment happens.

So, which one is more productive? More disciplined? Is Person A or Person B going to do better in the long run?

Hopefully this example has nudged you toward a potential answer: It really depends on what the task is!

In this section, we're going to see that daydreaming, doodling, and directionlessness are not a problem to be solved, and what's more, they may constitute a superior way of working—for the right tasks, that is.

"Hyperfocus" involves intense concentration on an activity for an extended period, and it's the strategy used by Person A. Here, "hyperfocus" involves intense fixation on a single task for an extended period. The ability to sustain attention on one task is one surefire way to increase productivity, learning, and power. It's also a great way of cutting stress, believe it or not. Multitasking is a behavior not correlated to productivity, and it can actually drain you and stress you out. Much of the efficiency of hyperfocusing comes from not squandering your focus in many directions, but channeling it all toward one narrow target. Focusing on and completing one task at a time can lead to faster accomplishment, a stronger sense of achievement, and greater clarity and simplicity.

But sometimes, being a "machine" of this kind is not optimal. Instead, you want to be more like an artist, a dreamer, or an explorer. Here's where "scatterfocusing" comes in. "Scatterfocus" is a method that consciously allows the mind to wander and explore without the constraints of relentless focus.

This is where we allow a wandering interest and curiosity to roam freely. While hyperfocusing is like saddling up a powerful stallion and riding so it takes you exactly where you want to go, scatterfocusing is more like taking a slower horseback walk through a forest, reins loose, being carried along wherever the horse chooses. Who knows what you'll find?

Hyperfocus is great for clear, pre-defined tasks consisting of smaller subgoals that simply need to be tackled one at a time. This is the kind of approach best suited for difficult problem-solving, for studying, for drills and rote practice, for memorizing, and for analysis.

Scatterfocus, however, is best for those tasks that are generative—i.e., those that require a degree of creativity and innovation. Brainstorming new ideas, dreaming up plotlines for a novel, coaxing inspiration for an artwork or piece of music, or thinking carefully about a deep philosophical, aesthetic, or moral question. This is the best approach for those tasks that are by their nature undefined, and tasks that are outside the box and as yet unimagined.

As you can imagine, many worthwhile tasks in life actually require a mix of both approaches. The great Archimedes, the first to have a so-called eureka moment, solved a tricky science problem while in the bath doing something else . . . but he nevertheless followed this flash of insight with a solid bout of hyperfocused work.

The big idea here is that there is no point in demonizing a "lack of focus"—not when it can be so useful! Rather than thinking that work can only look like Person A's schedule, we can recognize that the brain is capable of many different modes of operation, and the best way forward is *what works*. If we get too attached to our vision of what a productive person looks like and what they do, we may be missing out on that other, equally valuable kind of thinking.

If we use too tight and controlled a mode of thinking when we should ideally be allowing freeform creativity, then we risk limiting ourselves and missing opportunities or important flaws in our thinking. On the other hand, if we are too unstructured and our attention fragmented, we risk dawdling and getting lost in abstraction, never taking concrete action or settling on any one idea. It takes skill, then, to become a kind of Person C, who is able to match their approach to the task at hand.

When you are meeting tight deadlines, solving complex problems, or completing crucial projects, use HYPERFOCUS.

To achieve hyperfocus, the process is straightforward—allocate dedicated time to a specific task, ensuring it gets your undivided attention. For those finding this challenging (i.e., pretty much all of us!), two techniques can help.

The first is one we have already covered: the Pomodoro Technique, or something close to the 52:17 method. Make sure that no single block of time, whether it's fifty-two minutes or twenty-five minutes, is being split between tasks. Commit to one task and one task alone, and use a written "parking lot" to keep track of anything that occurs to you during that time.

Incidentally, a meditation practice can indirectly increase your productivity for precisely this reason. The better you are able to ignore distractions and random thoughts and diversions, the more easily you can tether your focus to the task at hand. Imagine that any idea or demand that is not related to the task is simply like an annoying fly that lands on you. All you have to do is flick it away—and don't spend a second more of your attention engaging with it.

The other technique is called time blocking, and it involves using a spreadsheet or journal to create a detailed schedule, designating specific "blocks" of time for different tasks. The duration of these blocks varies based on the complexity of the task, allowing for focused energy and task accomplishment.

When you're creating art, composing music, or generating innovative ideas in general, use SCATTERFOCUS.

Now, for obvious reasons, there are few fixed "techniques" for scatterfocusing—the whole idea is to be as unprogrammed and unstructured as possible. Nevertheless, there are a few common ways to help you get into the right state of mind.

Doodling involves engaging with a pencil and paper, possibly using a flipchart, to visually represent ideas related to the task. By connecting concepts with arrows and exploring visually, doodling can reveal patterns and central ideas. Use a range of colors, switch between different pens and markers, and include random diagrams and drawings. You are not producing any of this for anyone's consumption, so don't be afraid to make a mess.

Freewriting, on the other hand, encourages continuous writing without pauses or edits, often with a set timer or commitment to completing a specified number of pages. The process can be quite meditative. Just make sure that your hand is always moving and the ideas are always flowing. Consciously tell your inner critic to take a back seat, and don't go back to read anything—just write. This technique helps clear the mind of initial thoughts, paving the way for more powerful and creative ideas to emerge.

Later, if you want to, you can decide how you'll process these notes and doodles, but try not to think of an outcome as you're creating.

Finally, don't underestimate the power of simply allowing yourself free, unscheduled blocks of time. This sounds like it would be pretty easy, but the fact is that most people are very conditioned to expect a *programmed* day, where every hour is spoken for, and it's a problem if you're not doing some definable thing at all times. They may embark on unstructured time with an agenda that actually gets in the way of things.

Genuine breaks and unstructured time are extremely valuable. Go for a walk, but don't plan where you're going ahead of time. Go into the kitchen and make a meal, but without a recipe, and without any preconceived ideas of what you're doing. Sit in a café and people watch for a while. Put your devices away and just sit and be for a moment. What occurs? Take it from there.

Find Your Creative Rhythm

Rhythm, defined as a regular pattern of movement or events, is crucial for creative geniuses. Mason Currey's investigation into the daily routines of creative achievers shows that maintaining a rhythm in daily work, play, and sleep contributes to sustained creativity and outstanding outputs in various domains.

Establishing a balanced, harmonious rhythm in your daily activities, including focused work, play, and adequate sleep, is essential for enhancing creativity. Following a regularly recurring sequence of events allows you to oscillate between periods of concentrated effort and relaxed, unfocused moments. This practice, advocated by Ralph Waldo Emerson, promotes integrating play into your routine.

Maintaining this rhythm over an extended period increases the likelihood of entering a state of flow, characterized by optimal performance during challenging but manageable activities. Flow is neither hyperfocus nor scatterfocus, but a sense of harmony in the way you are moving between the two. It's like music or dance: Timing matters!

In such a flow state, you are more likely to receive creative ideas from your subconscious mind or even the collective unconscious. You create a life with just enough structure and routine to automate unavoidable daily tasks, but you have enough flex and give to accommodate and nurture those flashes of creativity when they do occur. In essence, adhering to a harmonious rhythm in your daily life enables you to perform at your best, tapping into both your subconscious and superconscious states of creativity. In simpler terms: find your rhythm, embrace the flow, and your creativity will bring a little magic to each moment.

In his book *Daily Rituals: How Artists Work*, author Mason Currey attempted to find the average daily routine in those people considered top of their creative game, whether in the arts or the sciences. He found that they tended to work for around eight and a half hours a day (of which about six and a half constituted creative work), around eight hours for leisure and play, and around seven and a half hours for sleep. The many notable figures he studied varied enormously.

Some spent very little time working and plenty of time playing (Viktor Hugo spent around two hours a day working and the rest on sleep and leisure, while Honore de Balzac would regularly put in thirty-hour days); some exercised a lot, and others not at all (John Milton spent more than three hours a day exercising, while Benjamin Franklin and Vladimir Nabokov did none); some had ordinary day jobs (Mozart,

Kurt Vonnegut), while others did not (Darwin and Picasso).

Through this variation, however, the overall average ratio of work-play-sleep was around 8:8:8. What these people had in common was also the fact that they tended to move through the same, predictable flow each and every day, moving from one activity to the next, mixing up different kinds of work, and mixing work with play.

How do you know what *your* flow is?

Here are a few steps to find out.

Step 1: Keep a detailed track of how you're spending your time for one full week. Note what you're doing and for how long. If it makes sense to do so, distinguish between different kinds of work—i.e., paid day job, main work, secondary work, admin, special creative work, etc. These categories may change over time. Also track how many hours are going to sleep, exercise, leisure time, play, and other life duties, such as admin, community work, family obligations, childcare, and housework (these last three were notably absent from Currey's analysis).

Step 2: After a week, try to average out the figures you've found and construct a twenty-four-hour timeline that represents your typical daily rhythm. Depending on your schedule, you may need to have two or more to reflect the fact that it changes slightly on weekend days or during holidays, for example.

Step 3: Analyze and reflect. How does your timeline compare to the average given by Currey? Are you surprised by anything?

Step 4: Design your ideal timeline. Depending on how effective you currently feel and how well you're able to access your own flow state, you may have identified a few areas of potential improvement. Perhaps you need more sleep and more play. Perhaps the ratios are fine, but the order of activities could be shuffled around. Perhaps you need to make intervals shorter or longer.

Step 5: Commit to one small action to bring you a little closer to your ideal timeline. Make sure it's something small, because you will need to consistently maintain the change not just for today but for every day after that. Take some time to experiment and see how things feel. You can measure your progress in some of the ways already described, but you can also ask your gut how natural and easy the flow feels. You might not arrive at the optimal flow on the first try, but you'll know you're getting closer when you have a schedule and rhythm that feels both comfortable and challenging.

Don't Worry about Other People's Rhythms

Occasionally, people will share their daily schedules or those of some celebrity in an attempt to make a point about how we should *all* structure our time. Maybe you'll learn that some famous entrepreneur gets up at 4 a.m. each morning or that some impressive influencer has a green smoothie at 11 a.m. every day no matter what. You can safely ignore all of this!

Other people's ideal flow states say nothing about yours. They are different people with different constitutions, different goals, different strengths and weaknesses, different contexts, different curses and blessings. If you get overly hung up on trying to emulate someone's nightly yoga routine, for example, you miss out on the opportunity to discover for yourself what actually works in your life. No matter how healthy someone else's schedule appears, if it doesn't work for *you* as the individual you are, then it won't be healthy.

Certain techniques and methods have been inspired by observation and research, but even this can change with time. For example, the 52:17 technique was originally presented in a 2014 *The Muse* article, and opposed the older Pomodoro Technique by claiming that the optimal time block was not twenty-five minutes but closer to double this amount. Funnily enough, just eight years later, the original creators of the 52:17 technique claimed that new findings suggested the best ratio to be 112:26—more than double their own original claim!

All of this is to say that at the end of the day, there are no magic numbers or secret hacks; what matters is your ability to maintain self-awareness and continually experiment and adjust based on the results you get in your real, actual life—not someone else's life. If there is anything to be learned from ultra-productive, creative, and disciplined people, it's probably to take responsibility for yourself and to experiment. Keep learning and keep curious. Take the lessons in this book, apply them, and see what works and what doesn't. Not only will you get more done and be more creative, but you'll live a happier, more balanced, and more authentic life, too.

The Daily Highlight

Have you ever reached the end of a day and felt absolutely exhausted, and yet at the same time, can't shake the feeling that you've done nothing at all? Have you ever done your absolute best to stay on top of tasks and worked as hard as possible, only to still feel a vague sense of failure, as though you haven't really "moved the needle"?

Our final section concerns a potential emotional roadblock that is difficult to name and put a finger on, but is sadly all too common, especially for those of us who work at desks in front of screens (i.e., most of us).

When we set productivity and discipline goals for ourselves, the impulse is usually coming from a deeper underlying emotional craving: What we really want is a happy, meaningful life that's full of vitality and success. However we envision it happening, this life is one where we feel like we are useful people who are able to contribute to the world . . . and have those contributions recognized and even rewarded.

Sometimes we can reach every single one of our productivity targets and discover at the end of the day that we still somehow feel empty or unfulfilled. The reason is that we did not actually address this deeper emotional craving. You may certainly be able to coax and train yourself into working hard, but merely being busy is seldom a long-term goal.

In the book *Make Time*, Jake Knapp and John Zeratsky highlight what they call the busy bandwagon. You're always hustling, always rushing from one task to the next, always optimizing, and when one goal is reached, the next is already in place. It's all go, go, go, and in the process of this relentless, machine-like hurry, you quickly lose any sense of joy or satisfaction in your own work.

Knapp and Zeratsky offer their "daily highlight" trick to counter this tendency. It involves selecting a crucial and meaningful task, such as writing an article, editing a video, researching a client's strategy, or exercising, and scheduling it on your calendar. It's not the tasks in themselves, but the sense of purpose, joy, and accomplishment you'll feel having done the task. It's a common trope that at the end of life, people lie on their deathbeds and look back, seeing only the most important, most special parts—the parts that defined the time they spent living. In a much, much narrower way, we can see each day like this. When the day is over, what will we want to look back on with pride, satisfaction, and a feeling of completeness? What task being ticked off the list will give us the richest sense of meaning and purpose?

Then you work backward and plan your day according to this anticipated highlight. This chosen activity is protected, ensuring that when the time comes to do it, it receives your full and dedicated attention. By focusing on something that feels real and important, you not only give yourself a sense of purpose and direction, but you make yourself more resilient when it comes to managing challenges and setbacks. The daily highlight encourages **intentionality** and concentration on how time is utilized throughout the day. This is the exact opposite of that busy-but-unsatisfied feeling.

If someone asks you what the highlight of your day was, what would you like to answer them? That some pointless and aggravating task was the main event? Or perhaps that there wasn't a highlight at all?

If you consistently and successfully apply productivity tips and tricks and find that you are disciplined and yet still not really *satisfied*, then this may be your missing piece.

To apply the daily highlight technique to your own life, you need to consider three principles:

1. Urgency: "What's the most pressing thing I have to do today?"

Bear in mind, of course, that urgent is not always important! Identify tasks that demand immediate attention and must be completed today and no later. Avoid getting caught up in less valuable activities, such as spending excessive time on email responses or unproductive Zoom meetings. Doing so is setting you up for that awful feeling at the end of the day where you know you've been avoiding and procrastinating, and now you actually feel more dread and apprehension at the idea of doing the task. Putting urgent things off makes them bigger in your mind, not smaller.

Sure, these tasks are not going to light your world on fire, but completing them is satisfying since it's like clearing an annoying blockage. People often think that they procrastinate because they're tired and uninspired; more likely it's the opposite: They're tired and uninspired because they're procrastinating. That blockage is hogging and draining your attention, and when you just get it done, you may realize afterward what a rush of energy and freedom you feel. Instead of looking around for a pleasant distraction, realize that the positive feelings are actually embedded in that task you're avoiding, just waiting to be released!

2. Satisfaction: "At the end of the day, which highlight will bring me the most satisfaction?"

Focus on tasks that will provide a sense of personal satisfaction and contribute to your long-term mission, values, and goals. These things can and will change day by day. Acknowledge that these tasks may also be vulnerable to procrastination, as they often don't demand immediate attention like the urgent ones do. If you keep doing the *almost-urgent* tasks and keep putting off the enriching but less-urgent ones, you're actively engineering a life that feels like nothing but a joyless rush through a list of obligations.

Here, we should clarify what we mean by satisfaction—it is not the same as distraction, entertainment, pleasure, or relaxation. In fact, your most satisfying task may often be the most difficult, most demanding task on your list! The challenge is directly proportional to the sense of achievement you unlock by doing it. Feeling lazy or avoidant may make you try to convince yourself that gaming or doomscrolling for four hours is what you want, but keep reminding yourself of that point at the end of the day where you'll be looking back on what you've accomplished. Is this a task that merely feels good in the moment, or is it one that will genuinely create feelings of triumph?

One final thing: your highlight doesn't always have to be lofty and idealistic. There is plenty of satisfaction to be gained from "mundane" activities like deep cleaning your house or organizing your bookshelf. Simply notice how you feel after certain activities that you predict will bring you joy and purpose. If you consistently notice that, for example, meditation and journaling don't make you feel like you've done something with your day, then pay attention and experiment. What does make you feel that way? Can you try to make that the focus tomorrow?

3. Joy: "When I reflect on today, what will bring me the most joy?"

Prioritize tasks that bring you the most joy and happiness. Sounds simple, but again our modern living can sometimes confuse us. The things typically on offer as "treats" or rewards are seldom conducive to genuine joy—things like drinking, overeating, material consumption, distraction, or anything on the endless conveyer belt of addictive gadgets and substances out there.

Today, everyone knows about the importance of "self-care," but how often do we trudge through these tasks with exactly the same tedium we have for all the other items on our to-do list? Find a balance between efficiency and enjoyment in your day, acknowledging that not every moment needs to be optimized for maximum efficiency—and that includes recreational activities. Only you can say what genuinely makes you happy. When last did you laugh out loud? When last did you feel truly lucky to be living your life? When last did you feel full of love for someone or something, or even just a sense of calm contentment? Try to recall the things that triggered those feelings, and deliberately put them on the main pedestal in your life. Shine a light on them. A joyful, meaningful moment doesn't have to be prolonged to "make your day." Simply starting your morning with a good conversation or a run in the countryside with your dog may only take an hour, but set the tone for everything else that happens that day.

Trusting your instincts is key when picking your daily highlight—whether it's something urgent, joyful, or satisfying. Listen to your gut to decide what aligns best with your feelings for each day as it comes. This is not a "have to" situation but a "choose to" opportunity. A good rule of thumb is to go for a highlight that takes sixty to ninety minutes. Less than sixty may not let you get into the zone, while over ninety may be too much. This time frame strikes a balance—long enough for something meaningful yet reasonable to fit around the rest of your schedule. Ultimately, this is daily work—do not leave the things that are most meaningful, enjoyable, or important for later; *prioritize them for right now!*

In the beginning, choosing a highlight might feel a bit strange or challenging, and that's perfectly okay. It may seem like a backward way to do things. Over time, you'll get the hang of it, and the process will become more natural. Remember, there's no way to mess it up, and since it's a daily system, you can always adjust and try again tomorrow, right?

Your highlight isn't a magical fix, and deciding where to focus your energy won't happen automatically. Being **intentional**, however, is a crucial step toward making more time in your life. If you wake up and simply allow yourself to be taken along in the tumble of tasks that rush at you and relentlessly demand your attention, then you're setting yourself up for a day that's full, but not *full*. You need to pre-emptively decide on where to place your attention—that attention is like a spotlight shining down on a stage, singling out the single brightest, most important actor.

The spotlight might change as you actively choose to let certain things fade into the background occasionally. And it certainly isn't the only thing you will do that day. What matters isn't even the things you're focusing on—it's the fact that you are focusing. That you are taking responsibility for how you invest your time and energy. That you are choosing and are in control. That is what will strengthen you and make each day feel like it *means* something.

Summary:

- One of the most important things to manage is your own ability to self-regulate. Knowing how to manage inevitable negative emotions is key to overcoming obstacles—and often we are the obstacle!

- Use Tony Robbins's Rapid Planning Method (RPM) to quickly get focused and organized, but combine it with an understanding of the emotions that may derail each step—such as fear, overwhelm, apathy, self-judgment, demoralization, and inability to commit. Your approach needs to be
    - Results-Oriented (R): What do I really want?
    - Purpose-Driven (P): Why does it matter to me?
    - Massive Action Plan (M): How will I achieve it?
- Don't demonize daydreaming; instead, use freeform, unstructured time as a tool. Hyperfocus is great for difficult tasks that require deep work, while scatterfocus is more appropriate for generative, creative pursuits that are less defined. Try doodling, wandering, or simply following your own nose.
- By noticing and respecting your own creative rhythm, you work with rather than against yourself. Most people manage an 8:8:8 ratio of work to recreation to sleep, but what others do is less important than what works for *you*.
- If you are disciplined and organized but lack a sense of joy, purpose, or satisfaction, the missing element may be a "daily highlight,"

which is a single crucial and meaningful task that you deliberately choose to focus on each day. Ask what is urgent, what brings joy, and what will leave you with a sense of accomplishment once the day is over.

Conclusion

So, where does that leave us?

You may have found some of the material covered here quite obvious, while some of it may seem far less intuitive. The only way to tell if any of it is really *useful*, though, is to actively try it out in your own life.

We began our book considering the eternal contradiction that most people wrestle with: They want to be more organized, more disciplined, and more productive, and yet it's so hard to make these things real in your life. Hopefully by this point, you're convinced that there are (thankfully) no shortcuts and cheat codes, but something better: the chance to take responsibility for our lives, to *choose* to experiment, to find the value in challenge, and to stay open-minded enough to try something new . . . something potentially more difficult. Once you realize that this path is something that you can want for yourself, a new world opens.

The big surprise is that being disciplined, focused, and organized actually doesn't take any more effort than being lazy, unfocused, and ineffective. No, really! It does require, however, that we do something different and have the courage and curiosity to pour our work and attention into a new direction.

Let's return to our original principle:

Being successful, accomplishing your goals, and being disciplined and focused means applying your efforts to the things that are genuinely under your control.

Being uninspired, unfocused, and lacking purpose and motivation means applying your efforts to things that are not under your control and never will be.

Hopefully you've learned a few new ways to continually shift your focus onto what *can* be changed, and convinced yourself that with enough conscious intention and determination, you can change it. That may mean tiny, mundane changes to everyday life, or it could mean bigger, more serious changes to your overall life trajectory . . . or both.

Productive and disciplined people possess no superpowers; the only difference is that they've made the decision to be so. That's all. Once they make this commitment to themselves, the only thing that remains is how they'll get it done.

To recap:

- Take control of your time by considering the way you divide up the day—use the 52:17 method, the Pomodoro Technique, the four quarters method, and the twelve-week year plan. Make it all fit by constantly keeping the pickle jar theory at the front of your mind.
- Take control of your priorities by removing areas of overcommitment, creating a "parking lot" for distractions and interruptions, theming your days, and using a bubble sort method to rank the items on your to-do list.
- Take control of your output by using the 70:20:10 technique—i.e., quantity breeds quality, and make sure you're managing your energy levels and never repeating yourself.
- Take control of your environment by actively finding clarity and streamlining your why, what, and when. A to-don't list will also help you streamline your environment and make it easier to build

and maintain good habits for the long term.
- Finally, take control of your mindset and your emotions by learning emotional mastery. Set goals and tasks and purposely notice and work with negative emotions, rather than repressing them. Understand when to use hyperfocus and scatterfocus, and how to lean into your own personal rhythms. Finally, use the power of intention to pick a daily highlight, and make that your day's focal point. This is the path to a day that feels more joyful, satisfying, and meaningful.

When you are disciplined, you no longer crave an easy life with quick rewards. Instead, you enjoy spending effort and overcoming challenges. That's because you know that every time you practice your power to choose, to experiment, and to set conscious intentions, you are strengthening that power. And then, discipline is no longer something you're doing, but something you are.

Summary Guide

CHAPTER 1: TAKE CONTROL OF YOUR TIME

- Julia Gifford has found that the most productive people tend to follow a cycle of working for fifty-two minutes and then taking a break for seventeen minutes. This approach can be combined with the classic Pomodoro Technique, which suggests a twenty-five-minute work period with five minutes' rest in between.
- The numbers are not what matters—what you do with them counts. When you plan your time effectively, less work can actually mean more work.
- The four-quarter method encourages you to divide the day up into defined quarters—morning, late-morning, afternoon, and evening—so that each new segment is a fresh opportunity to start again. Schedule defined task categories for each window, e.g., always exercise in the first quarter.
- The twelve-week year plan helps you break down the year into more manageable, medium-term chunks in the same way. It emphasizes a shorter execution cycle, which brings benefits such as increased

predictability, greater focus, and improved goal structure, plus more opportunities for course correction and adjustment.
- Finally, the pickle jar theory is an extended metaphor that helps explain how you can fit your tasks in order of their priority, given the finite amount of time you have each day. By placing your "rocks" into the jar *first* and then fitting in pebbles, sand, and water in the remaining space, you ensure everything fits and that you are never devoting time to insignificant tasks at the expense of your priorities.

CHAPTER 2: TAKE CONTROL OF YOUR PRIORITIES/FOCUS

- When you take control of your priorities, you are consciously choosing what you value and where you want to spend your effort, attention, and energy. Often, procrastination and lack of productivity is actually because we're overcommitted and fracturing our focus. Elizabeth Grace Saunders's "anti-overcommitment formula" is a tool to help you strategically measure where you're spending yourself, and make adjustments according to what you most value.

- Distractions, diversions, and interruptions are an inevitable part of life. But we don't have to respond to them. If you're in the middle of focused work, use a "parking lot" journal to note down intrusive thoughts and return to them later—if at all. This method can also be used to manage overthinking and rumination.
- Day theming is a way to stay focused and involves assigning each day a broad category or theme and committing to prioritizing those tasks and activities that match that theme. This allows you to cut down on that little loss of productivity and focus every time you switch tasks.
- Reorienting toward your priorities is work that needs to be done continually. If your to-do list is growing out of control, use a "bubble sort" to make sure the most important tasks bubble to the top and get done first. Be careful about falling into an "everything is an emergency" cycle, and recognize the difference between urgent and important, addressing things in the following order:
    - Important and urgent
    - Important and not urgent
    - Unimportant and urgent
    - Unimportant and not urgent

CHAPTER 3: TAKE CONTROL OF YOUR OUTPUT

- We are not in control of how naturally talented we are and cannot always guarantee that our work will be brilliant or amazing. What we can do is commit to consistency in our actions. By following the 70:20:10 technique, we understand that quantity breeds quality, and that if we just keep producing, eventually the brilliant and amazing will come: approximately seventy percent of what we produce will be mediocre, twenty percent will be poor, but ten percent will be something special. Consistency means continually creating and continually choosing to learn from what we do, whether it works out well or not.
- Perfectionism is extremely toxic and will undermine your efforts, especially if it lowers your tolerance for failure or the awkwardness that is part of every learning journey. Successful people do not fail less!
- How you manage your time and attention is extremely important, but energy matters too. Pay attention to your own unique energy patterns and rhythms, and work with rather than against your body. Set limits for yourself to preserve your energy rather than

deplete and exploit yourself as a resource. Recognize, too, that there are different types of energy and consequently different ways to be fatigued; understanding this means you can address tiredness and burnout correctly. Set daily minimums and maximums and honor them no matter what.
- Finally, don't repeat yourself (DRY). Pay attention to any repetitive tasks and use automation, delegation, or templates to make sure you're not doing the same task over and over.

CHAPTER 4: TAKE CONTROL OF YOUR ENVIRONMENT

- It's easy to make excuses and blame the environment around us for why we can't be more disciplined, but although the world influences us, we can also influence it. If we find that we are lacking clarity, then it's time to make the environment around us clearer by asking
    - Why are you doing the task?
    - What exactly are you doing?
    - When will you do it?

    This will give you focus and direction and stop you from getting hung up on reasons why you can't act.

- To better understand **why** you're doing a task, or why a problem is occurring, use the "five whys" technique. If motivation and passion are lacking, check in on your higher-level purpose.
- To better understand **what** you're doing, set both SMART and NICE goals to bring the dream to reality, especially if you're having trouble with losing momentum.
- To better understand **when** you will do a task, schedule tasks in your calendar and be patient!
- A to-don't list is a list of tasks you never do, and it's a way to manage your environment and take responsibility for your values and principles, rather than blaming the distractions.
- Build a "good habit machine" so your environment is actively and automatically making your desired behavior more likely. Give yourself frequent opportunities for both internal and external rewards to reinforce behavior. Be mindful of the progress indicators you're using, chart your progress, and regularly reflect on your progress.

CHAPTER 5: TAKE CONTROL OF YOUR EMOTIONS AND MINDSET

- One of the most important things to manage is your own ability to self-regulate. Knowing how to manage inevitable negative emotions is key to overcoming obstacles—and often we are the obstacle!
- Use Tony Robbins's Rapid Planning Method (RPM) to quickly get focused and organized, but combine it with an understanding of the emotions that may derail each step—such as fear, overwhelm, apathy, self-judgment, demoralization, and inability to commit. Your approach needs to be
    - Results-Oriented (R): What do I really want?
    - Purpose-Driven (P): Why does it matter to me?
    - Massive Action Plan (M): How will I achieve it?
- Don't demonize daydreaming; instead, use freeform, unstructured time as a tool. Hyperfocus is great for difficult tasks that require deep work, while scatterfocus is more appropriate for generative, creative pursuits that are less defined. Try doodling, wandering, or simply following your own nose.
- By noticing and respecting your own creative rhythm, you work with rather than against yourself. Most people manage an 8:8:8 ratio of work to recreation to sleep, but

what others do is less important than what works for *you*.

- If you are disciplined and organized but lack a sense of joy, purpose, or satisfaction, the missing element may be a "daily highlight," which is a single crucial and meaningful task that you deliberately choose to focus on each day. Ask what is urgent, what brings joy, and what will leave you with a sense of accomplishment once the day is over.